THE
UNEXPECTED ENEMY

D1461438

The Unexpected Enemy

A Muslim Freedom Fighter Encounters Christ

*Ghulam Masih Naaman
with Vita Toon*

Marshalls

Marshalls Paperbacks
Marshall Pickering
3 Beggarwood Lane, Basingstoke, Hants, RG23 7LP, UK
A subsidiary of the Zondervan Corporation

First published in 1985 by Marshall Morgan & Scott Ltd.

British Library CIP data

Naaman, Ghulam Masih
   The unexpected enemy: a Muslim freedom
fighter encounters Christ.
   1. Converts from Islam
   I. Title   II. Toon, Vita
   248.2'46   BV2625

   ISBN 0-551-01266-8

Typeset by Brian Robinson, North Marston, Bucks.
Printed in Great Britain by Hazell Watson & Viney Ltd,
Member of the BPCC Group, Aylesbury, Bucks.

Dedication

To our beloved daughter, Khulda, and to all daughters whose character and way of life are repositories of the honour of our Saviour Jesus Christ, the Son of God, in whose service I have been for the past thirty-one years. When my wife, Daisy, and I asked the Lord for a memorial to our simple witness to Him, He gave us Khulda.

Contents

Introduction

I have hesitated for a long time to write the story of my conversion to Jesus Christ. My motives have been mixed. I did not want to write it down for personal gain. So many 'testimonies' are often embellished with this end in view. And even one's purest motives can be tinged with 'sin'—a desire for self-gratification and self-glorification. I have always disliked a boastful spirit.

And yet I felt compelled to write. God has become real to me and I know that He acts within our world. I give Him all the glory. By putting down in a simple, straightforward way my story of how He brought me to Christ, I hope that His name alone will be exalted.

Furthermore, a written account speaks for itself. It will prevent me from changing details in it to suit different audiences. I shall no longer be tempted to tailor my reply to questions to meet with the approval of the person I am addressing.

To abandon anything that one holds dear in this world is almost a sacrificial act. A man may abandon his ambition, even his native country. But to abandon one's ancestral faith is greater still. And when that faith or religion is Islam then the magnitude of such a step becomes clear. I hope that others who may be called upon to take a similar step may be encouraged by the following pages.

I am grateful to Bishop Michael Nazir Ali of Raiwind, Punjab, for translating into English the short Urdu edition of the story of my conversion and ministry. This material, together with further information gained from personal interviews in my home in Sukkur, Sind, has been carefully woven into this longer English edition by Vita Toon, whom I count as a good friend. She has done a fine job for me.

I would also like to thank the Rev. Jim Hewitt for doing a quick translation and for carrying on the work of the late Canon R. W. F. Wotton who first brought my story to the attention of the Publisher.

Ghulam Masih Naaman
Sukkur. July 1984.

1: My Muslim Home

December 6th, 1949 was a very cold night. I remember it vividly for it has left an indelible mark on my memory. It was the night death stared me in the face. There was no obvious way of escape. This was to be my last night in this world. My family, my brothers and their friends had decided that very evening to put an end to my life. They were frustrated and desperate. There seemed to be no other way out of the shame and disgrace I had brought upon them. On the following morning, under cover of darkness, they would cut my body up in pieces, put the pieces in a sack and entrust it to the River Ravi so that the whole shameful business might be finished with. Directly after the evening meal I was stripped of all my clothes, except for a vest and a loin cloth, so that, numbed by the cold, I would be unable to offer any resistance to my executioners. I was put into a small, dark room with no windows. The door was shut and then locked from the outside.

As I sat on the floor in that cold, dark room my feelings were in a turmoil as I contemplated my fate. Here were my own flesh and blood about to murder me. How could such a situation have arisen where the murder of one member of a close and caring family becomes a necessary evil? For you to understand what led my family to this drastic step I need to take you back to my early years in order to show the strengths, weaknesses, loyalties, and failures of a Muslim home. Not that this information will lessen in any way the enormity of this dreadful plan for there cannot be any valid excuse for it. I believe that it is a sign of weakness, when, in cold blood, one group of people seeks to destroy the life of another. But I want you to see what can happen when a man changes his normal allegiance and rejects a noble inheritance.

We were a Muslim family of eight. I had four older brothers and a younger brother, Mohammed Ramazan. I was born in Jammu, Kashmir, where my mother had gone for a short holiday but our ancestral hometown was Zaffarawal in Sialkot. Our ancestors had originally come from Mongolia. They had been a landowning and wealthy people. This tradition continued right down to my father who was himself a landowner. We had rich farming land near the River Nala Dek on which we grew wheat. The Dek, which ran fast and full during the rainy season watered what was at one time unirrigated land on its banks. It enabled us to produce so much wheat that we never had the need to buy any. We were a very fortunate family who never had to experience want or deprivation of any kind. Most of the work on the farm was done by servants. I do not recollect ever seeing my father do any work. When my brothers were old enough they took over the running of the farm.

My brothers were much older than myself. After the birth of my four elder brothers, my mother did have other children but they all died in infancy. My birth and survival were seen as a miracle and I still carry on my body the mark which signifies it. My mother longed for another child. She was a devout Muslim but she retained a belief in goddesses which she inherited from our ancestors. Like most women whose desire to have a child is frustrated, she resorted to the only means she thought would realise her intense desire. She went up into the hills in Kashmir where there was a shrine of a goddess. She promised the goddess that if she had a son she would dedicate him to her and every year she would bring him to the shrine. As a sign that I belonged to the goddess she had my left ear pierced and a gold ring put in it.

You do not need much imagination to guess what this symbol of my belonging did for me at school. In addition to the taunts of my friends it was a gift to the other boys whenever I was involved in fights. The ring was what their little hands reached for at the first opportunity. Thus the sign of my miraculous birth and preservation from death held great pain and embarrassment for me. Later on in my life I did come to believe that a divine hand had been laid upon me but I also discovered that it was not the hand of the goddess but the hand of the living God.

My paternal uncle took pity upon me, however. He called me one day and gently took off the offending ring. How relieved I was! But my mother was deeply upset. She was most distressed as she truly believed that I would die. The ring was a kind of talisman, guaranteeing me the protection of the goddess. Without it, I was exposed to danger and even death. My uncle again came to my rescue: 'You will not

13

die,' he reassured me. My mother was just being superstitious. When she asked me to go to the shrine I politely refused. I was about nine years of age. As the days went by and I didn't drop dead, I was genuinely delivered from any fear there might have been at the back of my mind. Since then I have never experienced fear even in the most dangerous situations. I did however, experience grief when my younger brother Ramazan suddenly contracted pneumonia and died within a few days.

I was still a young boy when my four elder brothers were married. We all lived in the same house. It was a large house with eight bedrooms and a big hall. My brothers had separate rooms for their wives and children. We shared everything, a joint family so typical of the social structure in the India of that time. In a town or village community this was an essential element for it meant that all members of the family had guaranteed security. Each member of the family, whether he was well or handicapped, whether he worked or not, shared jointly in the common property and inheritance.

Our household was a full and happy one with a gentle mother and an affectionate father. It shone with our mother's care and the sisterly love of my brothers' wives. I always called my sisters-in-law 'sisters'. My father taught me both to call them and to treat them as sisters since I had no real sisters of my own. In any case we loved each other so much that it would have seemed unnatural for me to do otherwise.

In a household with four daughters-in-law, it might be expected that disagreements and arguments would be the order of the day. But it was not so in our home. Mother was a kind and gentle woman and the atmosphere we breathed was one of love and understanding. It was from my mother that I learnt early in life the value of service for others. 'To live for myself,' she said, 'makes me no different from animals. We can only prove ourselves to be true human beings if we live for others.' I saw her live out this principle even in circumstances which might have cost her her life. Her attitude and example made this the very foundation of my own life. Despite the darkness which at one stage threatened to engulf me, I never really departed from this foundation. It was the bedrock of my life.

My father had been a military man and held a Viceroy's commission with the rank of Subedar (a native officer in the Indian army, corresponding to the rank of Captain) in the First World War. During the years leading up to and after the First World War, Indian nationalism had not reached the stage where there was strong opposition to joining the army under British control. India was still very much an intrinsic part of the British Empire and even fighting overseas was regarded as an honourable occupation. My father cherished his memories of the War. He had a fund of stories to fire our starved imagination. And he did not have to compete with television or radio. We simply loved to listen to him telling us tales about the army's exploits, especially of the campaigns in which he was engaged in Africa. On one occasion he said that they had had no rations for weeks. They had to resort to boiling the leather of their shoes to provide food for themselves. Father instilled into me a love for heroic tales. Indirectly, he taught us that a man should identify himself in this

15

world by doing something very special. One must try to do something extraordinary with one's life. People should be able to recognise our abilities. We should not advertise them aggressively but act in such a way that our talents could be honestly evaluated. This kind of attitude was to have far reaching consequences in my life. Lacking fear as I did, and wanting to excel in life, it led me into some exciting but dangerous adventures.

My father was a public spirited man. If anyone was oppressed or so poor that he could not afford to obtain justice, then my father was always ready to do what he could do for him by seeking redress through the courts. He himself never took any litigation or law suit of his own to court. As a landowner, he must have had several occasions when he could have done so. Even soldiers in receipt of a pension used to turn to him to deal with their affidavits. My father was a kind and compassionate man. Because of this he was greatly respected in the neighbourhood and held a high place in the community. He loved entertaining; there were always guests in our home. On one occasion this generous spirit led him to welcome into our house the murderers of his own brother. His brother had been involved in a land dispute and a group of people had killed him. Afterwards this group fled, seeking somewhere to hide; unwittingly, they came and hid in a small shed my father had built in the fields. Not knowing of their foul deed my father invited them into the house and gave them a meal. Later, his brother's friends who were pursuing this murderous group arrived and denounced them. When my father learnt of his brother's death he was most upset. But to everyone's surprise he was not angry with the murderers. He was always a caring person and never harboured resentment against anyone. He believed he had done the right thing in his innocence.

Father derived his strength of character and attitude to people from his religious faith. He did not care much for the externals of religion and distrusted the Maulvis (the religious teachers of Islam). He disliked public worship and said his prayers privately. In fact he was a mystic.

Mysticism in Islam, or Sufism (direct communion of the soul with God), was probably modelled upon Christian hermits who were scattered in the deserts of Egypt and Arabia. The movement owes its continued recognition in the development of Islam to Al-Ghazzali who died in A.D. 1111. In its earliest stages Sufism was characterised by great devotion, humility, and asceticism, i.e. severe self-discipline and self-denial. Obedience to God was seen as something which must spring from the heart. A loving response was what God required and not mere observance of external laws. In their search for purity and personal experience of God the early mystics stressed the importance of prayer and contemplation and enjoyed the ecstasy of knowing God's love for them. Because of this love they were able to love God and respond obediently to Him. Only later did they employ external means (such as drugs and music) to stimulate a state of ecstasy. My father's mysticism remained a deliberate attempt to cultivate a personal relationship to God. It never developed into a longing for a mystical union with God. As a result he did not have to resort to the use of drugs, music, dance, or incantations to induce the mystical state. It remained on a moral plane which governed and informed his whole life.

In the home he was a very gentle person, greatly concerned with our welfare and especially our education. My brothers and I were educated in a school which was two miles from our home. To make it easier for us our father had a house built near the school in Zaffarawal so that it would be easier to get to school during term time. I started going to primary school when I was five. At this time I also started to go to the mosque which was near to our house. Every Muslim boy from the age of five was expected to go to the mosque once a week and learn to recite the Quran. Friday is the day for devotions for Muslims. Every Friday, along with my Muslim friends, I made my way to the mosque, the centre for congregational worship and also for instruction. While the Imam or prayer leader said the prayers, we all prostrated ourselves at the appropriate times, following his example. Usually he would give a short address in which he explained some aspect of the Prophet Muhammad's teaching. It was not always easy to understand him but our religious leaders made sure that we learnt our faith. There were special times when we had to go to the mosque for instruction. Thus, from my earliest years the basic tenet of Islam was instilled into me; *La ilaha illa Allah: Muhammad rasul Allah. (There is no god but Allah, and Muhammad is his Prophet.)*

My primary school headmaster had tremendous influence on me. He was a good poet, an orator, a writer, and a gifted musician. It was due to his encouragement that I began writing poetry myself. This has been a source of great delight to me

18

throughout my life. My notebook is never far from me, whether on the train or bus. I loved to play the harmonium but I was not allowed to play it at home. My headmaster persuaded me to go to his house and play there. Many years later, when I started going round the villages on foot or bicycle as an evangelist, I bought a harmonium for fifty rupees, and played it at the services I took. In retrospect, I can see the hand of God was upon me from my earliest years. He was preparing me for the life of service I would be called to live. The fact that He was concerned with me, and with even the smallest details in my life now fills me with wonder. He is truly a great God.

I spent four years in primary school. By the time I was nine, my brothers left home. Two went to Jammu and two went to Lahore. It was now time for me to go to High School. Although I had a great love for reading and writing poetry, I did not have much interest in academic work, but my family were determined that I should apply myself to it. The school they chose for me was in Jammu in Kashmir. It was the Maharajah Ranbeer Singh High School. In many ways it was a privilege for me to go there since this school was specially set aside for the sons of the rajahs or ruling families. The rajahs were the warrior kings who conquered and established themselves as rulers in various parts of India. There were twenty-two rajahs in Kashmir during this period. I was the only Muslim student in that school. Muslims were not allowed in it, only Hindus. Because my father had been in the army and had some influence he persuaded the headmaster to take me. People always found it difficult to refuse my father's requests although he was not an aggressive man.

This school offered a kind of pre-military training as befitting the sons of warrior kings. Horse riding featured prominently. I loved it. I also enjoyed shooting. My father's 'Greener Gun' was very light and I could cope with its recoil. I remember spending a lot of time with it whenever I had the opportunity at home. This was a much more pleasant thing to do than going to fetch the milk from the Haveli (a kind of manor house) every morning, a little task which had to be taken over by the servants because I refused to do it. The hunt interested me more than studies. Diligence and hard work had not yet become a part of my character. Besides, the purpose of this kind of education was not clear to me. The sons of the rajahs were being prepared for their future professions; some were commissioned as junior officers in the army and others went into public service. But what was I being prepared for? While I enjoyed life in the school I had no idea where it would lead me.

This was essentially a school for Hindus. Consequently, we observed some of the practices of Hinduism. I too began to look forward to getting up early in the morning to go to prayers. We had to memorise perfectly, word by word, the Mantras of the Hindu scriptures. These enshrined the basic teachings and precepts of the religion. As a religion, Hinduism did not attract me but what I learnt gave me invaluable understanding of it. I also had to learn Hindi which I speak fluently to this day.

There was however, one big gap in my education at the high school. I did not learn anything about Islam. I was happy enough about it, but my late brother Khuda Bakhsh was not. Because of the death of father, he had now taken over the responsibility for my education. He made me leave the school and enter as a boarder at Jammu Islamiyyah High School. This turned out to be an orphanage rather than a boarding school! My brother was not deterred by this. So anxious was he for me to have more knowledge of Islam that it made not the slightest difference to him where I gained it.

I was not an enthusiastic boarder; I used to skip lessons and go home for meals at any time during the day when I felt like it and when I knew my brother would be away on business. My 'sisters' did not expose me. Inevitably the school made formal complaints. This soured the relationship between myself and my brother. He was paying for my education and here I was, making little use of the opportunity he was working so hard to provide.

This situation worsened as a result of a deeply personal relationship I had formed with a young girl. During one of the vacations I had gone to a village near Srinagar, where we had a piece of land. There I met Salima and fell passionately in love. From the moment I set my eyes upon her I was captivated. She was the daughter of the family who tended our land. They were distantly related to us. We became good friends and used to meet frequently and go for walks. I didn't realise that the attraction was mutual until the day before I was due to leave. We were together. Suddenly she began to weep. She didn't want me to leave. This touched me deeply and our love for each other grew stronger every minute. The next year when I returned to this place, I found that she had grown more beautiful. However, I could sense a change in her. She tried to avoid the kind of intimacy we had had previously and seemed rather distant. She

21

reassured me that her love for me was greater than ever; she had missed me terribly. I was puzzled. What could be wrong? Our relationship had been a pure one.

We simply enjoyed being with each other. Real love can be experienced without sexual intercourse. I learnt early in life that sexual intimacy can destroy a beautiful relationship. One must reserve that for one's life partner, and only after marriage. Alas, marriage between us was not to be. Her family had sensed, and rightly so, that my family would never approve of such a marriage. Salima's family were not wealthy enough for ours. My family would never let such a union take place. At the back of my mind had lurked the fear that this would be the case, but I had not allowed myself to entertain it. However, I could not dismiss it any longer. My family made it quite clear that marriage to Salima was out of the question. Her fears had been horribly realised. My heart was broken but there was nothing I could do. The relationship between me and my family became strained further.

With my heart heavy with grief, I returned to school. But I just could not apply myself to my work. I was never very excited about work anyway. Now it seemed almost pointless. I was no longer happy there and I was not happy at home either. My family had deliberately and consciously spoilt my chance for real happiness. It was not long, however, before this unhappy state of affairs reached a climax.

During one of the periods when I skipped a lesson, my brother returned to his home in Jammu unexpectedly and found me in a nearby tea shop. Tea shops were common places of gossip and idleness. I enjoyed sitting there listlessly, watching the crowds. Suddenly, I was rudely awakened. My brother was standing by me. He demanded to know what I was doing in the tea shop when I should have been at school. Of course I had no satisfactory answer to give to him. He became angry. He saw a young boy who was no more than seven or eight years old working in the shop and seized the opportunity to disgrace me publicly. My brother called this young boy and began to question him. Child labour was not forbidden nor was education compulsory, so it was not unusual to see children working. Obviously his position contrasted sharply with my very privileged one.

'Sonny,' my brother asked, 'what time do you get up for work in the morning?'

'I get up about 3 o'clock in the morning, Sir, and I clean all the dirty dishes from the night before, scour the pots and pans for the morning purees (flat cakes) and halvas (batter pudding) and then I remain with the shop keeper all day.'

'What time do you go off to bed at night?'

'Never before eleven o'clock, Sir.'

My brother turned to me, his eyes blazing with anger. 'Look at this child, hardly old enough to leave his mother's side; he only gets four hours sleep a day. Let him be an example and a lesson to you. You do not study and you do not work. Be a man! Life can be extremely hard for those who throw its opportunities away.' With that he turned abruptly and left.

I was left confused and embarrassed. My life of idleness passed before my eyes and I was ashamed. My family had a good reputation. They were also very wealthy. I was becoming an intolerable thorn in their flesh. My dependent state with all its humiliation dawned upon me. I took my brother's words as a personal challenge and decided there and then that in my way through life I would rely entirely upon myself. I would not continue to live on the favours of other people. This new resolution did not, however, lead to a more zealous application to my work at school. Instead I grew disgruntled with everything. The tenth year examination was to be held in March. Just before this I ran away.

2: Who is this Jesus?

I was only sixteen years of age. World War II had begun and India was caught in a dilemma. How could India join in the war with the imperialist power which held the whole Indian sub-continent in subjection? Naziism was evil and must be condemned but for many Indians it represented merely an extreme embodiment of the same imperialism and racialism which held India in subjection. The Indian National Congress was loud in declaring that only a free India could join in the war against Germany. 'The people must be consulted', was its cry. The political leaders, however, were divided. They hated Hitler's aggression but were also hostile to the idea of helping Britain. Yet a subject nation cannot call the tune and when war broke out India found herself fighting on the side of the British.

Like most Indians I too shared the intense desire for Indian independence from British rule but I was too young to appreciate all that was going on in the world of politics and ideologies. My immediate concern was to find something to do. I was all alone. I could expect no help from my family nor did I want any. I was resolute in my determination to stand on my own two feet. The only effect of all the political turmoil upon me was to make it easy for me to join the Armed Forces. I was an easy recruit; I was a runaway. When therefore I applied to enter the Royal Air Force I had no difficulty. I answered favourably the few questions that were put to me and was enlisted as a FME—a Flying Mechanical Engineer—concerned exclusively with the maintenance and repair of aeroplanes.

My initial training took place in Lahore in the Punjab. Here I learnt aviation under instructors who were mainly American. They were very friendly towards us and not unnaturally my vocabulary became enriched with Americanisms.

My first posting was to Dum Dum airport in Calcutta. After a short period of instruction, I was sent to Burma and Rangoon. I did normal army routine work and, as this was a field area, we were on twenty-four hour duty. There was hardly any time for recreation but even when there was it wasn't always possible to enjoy what we were doing. I remember once we tried to work our film projector. Every time we began, there was a Japanese air raid. This happened four times in succession. In the end we didn't see the film. Sometimes we would walk several miles to see a movie. One night as I was returning from one such outing I heard some noises behind me. It was around twelve o'clock. At first when I turned around I didn't see anything because in those days we did not drive with lights on. Suddenly a jeep stopped beside me. The man inside offered me a lift and made me sit beside him. As his coat was flapping in the wind I caught sight of his uniform. To my horror, I realised that he was the area commander. This was such a shock to me I could hardly breathe. I feared that I was going to be court-martialled. He sensed that I was frightened and tried to reassure me. When we reached camp I got out of the jeep and thanked him. To my surprise and amusement he replied, 'You are welcome, Honey!'

I was later sent to the Air Force Academy in Calcutta. There I did a Master's degree in military intelligence. One of our teachers on administration said something which I have never forgotten. He used to say to us: 'Always win the confidence of your subordinates.' This became the guiding principle in my relationship with the men under me. I always tried to build up a personal relationship with them. Whenever anyone was in difficulty perhaps because of illness in his family, I would try to help in whatever way I could. In arranging for their leave I would sometimes give them money to help with their fares.

For me at this stage of my life the value of every human life did not depend upon one's colour, race or creed. Life is precious whatever the nature of the vessel it is contained in. Unfortunately, not everyone shared this view.

I never disobeyed the orders of my senior officers, nor would I allow my subordinates to disobey mine. During the war disobeying orders carried the death penalty. But I never made use of this punishment. If at any time a young subordinate did not obey my order then I tried to find a way of rescinding it honourably. I didn't see any point in throwing away good lives either by compulsion or by necessity. In this game of death their lives were just as precious as anyone else's.

I was still comparatively young but this did not

prevent me gaining promotion rapidly. In the early days of the war the Allied Forces received severe setbacks on every front. This critical situation was met by offering promotion to the most able men: some saw this move as a tactic to keep morale high, but my promotion was in no small measure due to the upbringing I had received from my respected father. Full dedication to my work, integrity and trustworthiness; these were the qualities which enabled me to prosper and succeed in every position. I did not tolerate dishonesty in myself and never in others. I would never put pressure on my subordinates without good reason, and would listen carefully to their legitimate requests. Thinking only of their convenience, I was sometimes even prepared to do a spell of duty for them myself. This was why the young men under my command were ready to shed their last drop of blood for me.

On the advice and recommendation of my respected senior Indian officers I became part of a combined group of the Intelligence Corps. At first I still continued with my own craft and trade but I was finally released from my own trade and began to receive specialised instruction in this particular area. I was not in any way anti-British but I could not help noticing that relationships in the Air Force were not very pleasant or desirable. Some of the British officers were very condescending in their attitude to the Indian officers. They regarded us as inferior and called us 'bloody Indians' and their language to us was not polite. Of course, we did not always distinguish between what was good or bad in their speech. I was once called to the Commanding Officer on some charge which I don't now recall. For some reason which I cannot explain in giving my statement I used language which I had heard spoken. The Commanding Officer was a Christian and listened very patiently. Then he said to me, 'Dear boy, tell me from where did you learn such beautiful English?' 'From fellow officers,' I replied. 'Next time,' he said, 'don't use such abusive language.' I felt so embarrassed.

There were greater problems which troubled me. I was very disturbed by the preferential treatment given to British Sahibs. Their lives seemed to be worth so much while Indian lives were devalued and could be dispensed with easily. This formed a wide gap between Indian and British officers, even those of the same rank. Discrimination was widespread. I don't suppose that attitudes here in the Air Force were any different to what they were in other areas. The British made no attempt to mix socially with the Indians. Many believed that one of the great joys of going to a place like Simla, that famous hill station in the Himalayas, was not only to get away from the heat but also from the native population! For me this attitude was shown in tragic circumstances from which I could not easily dissociate myself.

I had a close friend—Squadron Leader Surinder Singh. He lost his life as a result of this prejudice and preferential treatment. Our area Commander had been notified several times of some fatal defects in a certain bomber. One day he sent orders to our workshop that because of these reports, Surinder Singh would have to take this aircraft out on air tests himself. Surinder was prepared to go although he was rather apprehensive because of previous experiences. He took the aircraft and flew it in the appointed direction. We lost radio contact with him after about fifteen minutes. When a further fifteen minutes had passed we saw that an aeroplane was coming over the Bay of Bengal. It was Surinder. The land forces had not been alerted to provide cover for him and firing from the Japanese had blown away half his face and one of his eyes.

The second distressing situation arose out of the Bengal famine. It truly revealed human sinfulness and weakness at its worst. During 1943–44 Bengal, East and South India were devastated by famine. Epidemics followed the famine, especially cholera and malaria. This soon spread to other provinces. Conflicting accounts of the famine and its consequences were widespread. Unofficial accounts put the death toll at 3,400,000 but the official Famine Enquiry Commission which was set up concluded that 1,500,000 deaths occurred in Bengal 'as a direct result of the famine and epidemics which followed in its train'. Whatever the exact figures, no one could doubt that every day death was claiming thousands of lives. It is believed by many that this awful famine could have been averted; but the authorities revealed a sense of indifference and complacency I had never witnessed before. At first no one would believe the horrific accounts which were coming out of the devastated areas. Some authorities even accused those responsible for these reports as 'dramatising' the situation. The time came, however, when these reports could not be denied and the consequent wrangling over who was to blame only diverted attention from relief to self-justification.

The insensitivity of British officers was shown in all its nakedness during this crisis. Thousands were dying daily yet spare rations lay rotting in the government's ration depots. Malaria was a killer disease in those days, yet a vast supply of anti-malarial medicines remained unused in our medical stores. Utterly sickened by the insensitive behaviour of all around me, I began taking tea and sugar, rice and lentils from the ration stores and distributing them freely among needy people. I also gave away some anti-malarial medicines. I will relate later what price I had to pay for this activity. The only purpose in mentioning it here is to show that I saw life in all its degradation and poverty at very close quarters. Even the wealthy Indians, with all their accumulated wealth, could not buy food for themselves. People were reduced to exchanging their daughters' virginity for food. Of course there were those who did not fail to seize the opportunity to exploit their fellow human beings. Those who could lay their hands on them sold anti-malarial tablets for one rupee each! So low could man sink. Then there were those whom no human tragedy could touch. While the famine raged and the epidemics took their toll, revelry went on daily among both the English and the wealthy Indians in Calcutta. The rich with their petty squabbles and love of pleasure carried on as if nothing was happening.

My mind was thrown in turmoil over all this. My young mind was subjected to ideas and situations it could not easily cope with. Yet they sunk deep into me and created havoc. In many ways I could only react emotionally to all that was going on around me. My youthful years seemed to be speeding past me. I had to grow up fast in those circumstances. My own helplessness was brought home to me forcibly.

Together with a fellow Indian officer named Puran, I picked up two boys abandoned on the road and brought them to the camp. We kept them hidden in the hillside for more than six months. When the Commanding Officer got to know about this we were severely reprimanded. My colleague and I were prepared to pay any price to save the lives of these children but the affair did not reach that point. The children were sent to a refugee camp in some remote part of West Bengal. Perhaps the children are still there. We hoped that they might have met some good neighbours who would help them as we were powerless to do anything more for them.

How hard it was to swallow these emotions. 'Why is life here held so cheap?' I kept asking myself. 'How is human life to be evaluated?' 'Does no one really care?' 'If there is a God where is He in all this?'

I soon discovered that there is light in all the darkness. No one person or group of people is wholly bad. There is good in each one of us just as there is evil. It is true that the dominant attitude of the British officers towards the Indians was one of arrogant superiority, sometimes resulting in brutality. But there were those whose lives were shining examples of great goodness and Christian love. These were the people who truly sought to imitate their Master Jesus Christ and reveal the light and love of God. Their effect upon me was to plant within me a seed that would later grow and flower in full conversion.

One of these people was Group Captain Baxter. He was a young officer who was transferred to our No. 345 Wing. Like most of the British he was reserved but he was also broadminded. In his treatment of his subordinates we could see clearly the kind of person he was. He was neither patronising nor condescending to the Indian officers. He cared for our welfare. There was the time when the Indian staff requested separate cooking and eating arrangements. Muslim cooking requires special preparations and a special type of oven to cook the food. Our most urgent need was to have chulhas (ovens of clay) made for the new mess. It was agreed that we should have these but under the conditions in which we were living, it was not easy to see how our need was going to be met. You can imagine my amazement, and I may add, amusement, when I returned from the workshop one day to find that Baxter had got hold of a book of instructions and with its help was trying to construct an oven himself. My admiration for him grew. As I watched him I began to realise what great love for his men must be in his heart that he should want to construct our oven with his own hands. He obviously appreciated the nature of our request and was determined to see it fulfilled. It was a simple gesture but it moved me deeply.

In most eastern countries, it is a sign of acceptance and friendship if people share a meal together. Strangers know they are welcomed if they are invited to have a meal with the host. Baxter ate breakfast with us every day; something other British officers would never do. Again, this may seem a trivial thing but in the climate of foreign domination in which we lived, this was something special. It was a genuine act of friendship and comradeship and we all responded warmly to it.

Baxter was not a man to reprimand his men lightly or for trivial offences even when reprimand would have been appropriate. For example, some young men once turned up unshaven for breakfast. Instead of rebuking them, Baxter produced a blade from his own pocket and gave it to the men so that they could go and shave.

What impressed me most about Baxter, however, was his behaviour in times of raids. If there was a Japanese bomb attack while he was present, instead of going to the trenches for shelter he would say to all the men, 'Come on, lads. Let's go to the Chapel.' The Chapel was just a tent used for worship. We normally obeyed him. During these times in the Chapel he always did all the praying himself. The only part we had to play was to say 'Amen'. This happened two or three times. One day there was a particularly severe attack. We could see Japanese aircraft appearing in the sky. Soon the whole sky was full of planes and we started running to the trenches. Death seemed almost inevitable. Baxter shouted after us. 'Boys, it is no use running to the trenches; you won't be saved in there. Let's go to the Unit Chapel.' We all laughed nervously at this silly order. It was all right to go to the Chapel when there was a little raid. But this time the idea seemed ridiculous. Baxter however had a note of authority and assurance in his voice. 'I am going to pray to the Lord Jesus. You don't have to believe in Him or do anything. Just say "Amen" when I am finished.' Sceptical and reluctant we obeyed and entered the tent with him. We sat down, feeling rather sullen, amazed at this pathetic gesture in such a crisis.

As Baxter began to pray, he wept. His words still ring in my ears:

'Lord Jesus, reveal your strength and power
today.
Prove to these little ones that you are real.
For the sake of their loved ones and their
parents
Protect them from this attack today.
Let these men know that you are alive and
save not only man's body
But also his soul from destruction.'

While Baxter was praying a strange transformation
took place in this Chapel. Everyone became
absolutely silent. Stranger still, we couldn't hear
anything happening outside. We were only in a tent
yet there seemed to have been a blanket of silence
hanging over it.

When we eventually emerged from the tent, the
sight which greeted us was simply horrific. Pieces of
human flesh were strewn all around. The Unit which
was based on the other side of the canal had been hit
by several bombs. Heart-rending sounds and the
groans of young men reached our ears. In addition,
so many bombs had fallen into the canal right behind
the main mess that the water was boiling. Mud was
overflowing its banks and fog hung everywhere. In
the midst of all this destruction, there we were, safe
and sound. Dazed and shocked, we could not help
concluding that 'Baxter's Lord Jesus does listen to
prayer and save His people. He is truly alive.'

'Who is this Lord Jesus?' I wondered. As far as I
knew from the Quran he was simply a prophet, like
all other prophets. Yet people do not pray to
prophets after they are dead to ask for deliverance! I
had never heard of prayer in this fashion. It was so

35

simple and direct. When I was a little boy growing up in our hometown to please my Christian friends I used to go to the American Mission station which was there. What we enjoyed most was going into the missionary's house after the services to sing choruses with his wife and play with the many toys which they had. But during the services I never understood what he was saying or praying. He always shouted a lot. Baxter's prayer was an eye-opener for me. He seemed to be talking to a friend standing by his side. It seemed so easy. Was it really possible?

Little did I know at this stage in my life that one day this privilege would be mine. I too would have the joy of knowing this Lord Jesus as my Friend and Saviour.

3: Battles Within and Without

Shortly after our deliverance from Japanese bombing I was again working as a Flying Mechanical Engineer. But my work was curtailed by an accident which nearly cost me my life. I had an accident similar to that of my friend, Surinder. We had to repair damaged aircraft and after repairing them we had to test them out before delivery. One day I received orders from our Commanding Officer to test an aircraft because the work which had been done was not wholly satisfactory. The communication system did not seem to be functioning properly. I recalled what had happened to my friend. Half of his face had been blown away on such a test flight. But I had to obey orders. Along with another friend I took off. We were given thirty-three minutes to test it and come back. This aeroplane travelled at 300 miles per hour. When I was only thirty miles from the field workshop I was hit from the ground. I began bleeding. My friend Putan pushed me from the pilot's seat and took over the controls. We managed to land safely. I was taken to hospital, the 56th Indian General Hospital. The right side of my face (including my eye) was severely burned and damaged. When I arrived I was taken to casualty and given first aid. I was hardly conscious of what was happening, but I realised that there was difficulty in admitting me. Two days previously a bomb had fallen on the ward reserved for the British officers. Lying semi-conscious on the stretcher, I overheard a conversation between the Senior Medical Officer and two nurses. When they enquired what was to be done to me he insisted that he could not admit me into a general ward because I was RAF personnel. The nurses were very upset because they knew the extent of my injuries. One of them asked the Senior Officer, 'Which is more important? Rank or life?' They did not succeed in persuading him to admit me into the general ward but offered to look after me themselves in a room in the nurses' quarters.

I could not see where I was. Both my eyes were bandaged. I learnt of my situation from the conversations I overheard. For twenty days I lay in that room but I was not neglected. My two 'angels' saw to that. With their own hands they fed me and made sure all my needs were met. I do not remember what other medical attention I received. All I know is that from then on I have never been able to see properly with my right eye.

Early in the morning of the day when I had to leave hospital these two nurses came into my room and introduced themselves. They were Amber and Mary, two Indian nurses. I was curious to know why they had shown such love for me and cared for me when others seemed so indifferent. My ego was not inflated by their answer but I was stirred in the deepest regions of my being. 'The reason we attended you,' they said, 'is not because you are very handsome (they could hardly think this of me in my stricken

38

condition with eyes bandaged!) or because we are looking for a reward, but simply because we are Christians. Our Master suffered for man's salvation, and it is our duty to serve our fellow men in similar circumstances.'

I was overwhelmed by this simple confession. I wept so much that it seemed as if I would drown in the flood of my own tears. That these two nurses should have cared for me so compassionately in the name of their Lord truly humbled me. They comforted me and said, 'You must not cry; your wound is still fresh.' I bowed my head in a feeling of immense gratitude and dearly longed to kiss their feet. Once again I was confronted with the Lord Jesus in these two disciples of His. He seemed to be pursuing me in some way. I could not escape. In the midst of all the slaughter I was witnessing daily, and in the context of an apparent lack of concern for human life, here were some of God's people, caring and living for others. They were upholding another set of values similar to those my own mother had taught me. God's presence was surely with His people. Was He beckoning me in some way?

There was no time for such reflections to be prolonged. I was discharged and sent back to camp. On arrival I was told that I was relieved of my work as a field engineer and given light work to do. My job was to prevent service personnel, and particularly Air Force personnel from entering those areas of the city which were 'out of bounds'—i.e. red light areas. In this position I became well acquainted with the people living in these areas. This would seem to be an unlikely situation in which to encounter genuine love but this is precisely what I found.

There was a young airman in our field workshop called Philip Badri Nath. He was born in the province of Bihar. His presence provided us all with ample opportunities for rest and relaxation, for life with Badri was synonymous with fun and laughter. Camp regulations were often infringed with the excuse that so much enjoyment was to be found in Badri's company that no one had the heart to leave. But it was not his convivial nature which drew me to him. It was the sacrifice he was willing to make out of love for his Saviour. For this love transcended the fear of ostracism and degradation.

One morning I was ordered to inform Badri that he was being transferred to another workshop. He was deeply upset. He didn't want to go. When I questioned him he explained that there was a girl, Kumla, a prostitute, with whom he had fallen passionately in love. She also came from a disreputable family. I tried to reason with him by pointing out to him that to marry such a girl was contrary to accepted social practice, but Badri was adamant. He was not doing this lightly. It was an action which sprang from his deepest convictions. 'My religion is based on sacrifice. The Lord Jesus loved a wicked person like me and offered His own life as a sacrifice for the salvation for my soul. If He can receive someone like me, then it is my duty to accept sinful people whom the world despises.' This resolution and depth of character I was witnessing came somewhat as a surprise to me. Badri had given the impression of someone who was light hearted and carefree. Now he seemed like a totally different person. His high ideals shone like brilliant lights in darkness. Nothing I could say seemed to have any effect on him; his mind was made up. To him this proposed marriage was an act of sacrifice, almost a direct imitation of his Master's. Mr. Baxter understood. With his help I was able to explain the whole affair to the Commanding Officer and the order of transfer was rescinded. Kumla was invited to stay in the camp until the wedding which was performed by the area Chaplain. Later they both went to live in Badri's village. This to my mind was the ultimate act of bravery. He could easily have gone to a place where no one knew them but to go among his own people where there was bound to be criticism and disapproval took a lot of courage.

In the following days I could not erase these experiences from my mind. Baxter's quiet Christian life, Amber and Mary's kindness, and the practical example of self-sacrifice displayed by Philip Badri Nath. They kept going round and round in my mind and I was almost forced against my will to reflect upon them. Where did the grace and strength come from that would enable a man to defy social convention and prejudice to marry the girl he loved? These people believed they owed their lives to the sacrifice the Lord Jesus had made for them and they were allowing Him to direct and govern their lives. They did not simply believe a set of doctrines. All these ideas transported me into a different world—a world in which I could expect to see everyone loving and caring for one another. What a vision by which to live. But it was not mine. Perhaps it ought to be.

There was, however, no time to seek answers to the questions which were troubling me. In a world which was gradually becoming meaningless and purpose-less, I had glimpsed another one, a world in which human life was sacred and precious, and one's moral values were not being constantly eroded. But the inner turmoil which my experiences were creating within me was nothing compared to the greater turmoil which was engulfing our country. Politics invades one's existence whether one wishes it or not. The whole of the Indian subcontinent was on the verge of a great upheaval.

World War II ended in 1945. Peace had at long last arrived in Europe, but for the millions in India it was one of the bloodiest periods of her long existence. And this time it was not our foreign rulers who were directly responsible. It was religion. Religion became the rock upon which our people stumbled. Hindus and Muslims were no longer able to live side by side peacefully. The dream, vague though it might have been, that all Indians shared from time immemorial, of one India, united and peaceful, was shattered forever. Now they were caught up in a wave of bitter hatred for each other. Fear fuelled this hatred to an extraordinary degree. The scale of murders, riotings and arson which ensued must have baffled even the most cynical.

What a change this was to the world in which I was brought up. It was not as if Islam was a new religion. It arrived in India way back in 712. Despite occasional clashes, it was tolerated and coexisted peacefully with the Hindu religion already established and entrenched in the country. Only several centuries later did Islam become a political force when a descendant of Chengiz (Jenghiz) Khan captured Delhi in 1526 and established the Mughal dynasty. Even then Islam was still confined to the northern parts of India such as the United Provinces and Bengal. The Mughals did not attempt wholesale conversion of the population to Islam. The powerful class of Hindu Brahmins would not have let them even if they wanted to. While some among the Muslim upper classes were descendants of the Mughals, the masses of the adherents of Islam had been converted from the lowest strata of Hindu society. In the end the Hindu and Muslim masses were hardly distinguishable from each other. Both were found among the poorest and most exploited of the population.

How was it then that people, who for the most part, had lived peacefully together, should now harbour only hatred for each other? The answer lies in the political scene. Underneath all the schemes of the politicians was fear—that destructive and sometimes debilitating emotion. It seemed to have been at the root of all the problems. Muslims feared that in exchanging British domination for Hindu domination in an independent India, they would be putting themselves in a worse position. They believed that the Hindus could not be trusted to treat them equally and justly—and the Indian Congress was controlled by Hindus. The Muslims were also becoming more aware of themselves as a people with their own identity. The new Muslim middle class was beginning to assert itself. Although at first they avoided western education and thus blocked their own progress in trade and industry, they soon discovered that English education offered a good avenue into government service. The lure of such service proved powerful enough to overcome old resentments and prejudices and drag them away from their feudal ways. Thus they were now an eloquent and distinct group who saw that they could influence the destiny of their people. The Muslim League which was formed in 1906 was a deliberate and conscious attempt to safeguard Muslim rights. Even British policy changed and became more and more favourable to the Muslims.

Amidst the welter of political ideas absorbing the minds of Hindus and Muslims alike, one cry was beginning to sound loud and clear: Muslims must have a state of their own—Pakistan. Thus nationalist feelings fired the imagination of the Muslims. Once the idea had gripped the imagination of the masses it could not be eradicated. Added to this was a religious fervour which set the political scene ablaze. Earlier, the cultural heritage which Hindus and Muslims shared was enough for them to coexist peacefully. Now their religious faith, allied with intense nationalism, became the rock upon which they fell, dividing them irretrievably.

To establish some sort of peace in the country and quell the riots, the British Army was called upon to help the police. My part in all this was, however, short-lived. I was experiencing my own internal and external battle. Baxter was no longer with us. He had been transferred to some other station. One day after the evening meal I was suddenly arrested. The following day I was taken to an Indo-Chinese island called Bala Nakamatti situated in Singapore. I had no idea of the charges against me, but later learned they were connected with the Indian National Army. Let me explain.

When the Japanese conquered Burma and Malaya, they captured many Indian officers and soldiers. They persuaded these to form the Indian National

Army and dedicate themselves to the liberation of India from the British. Japanese support could be relied upon. The Indian National Army (INA) might have been used primarily for Japanese propaganda purposes but it had the support of a famous Bengali politician and former Congress Leader, Subhas Chandra Bose, who went to Japan in 1943. He was a fervent nationalist and saw in the war the chance of a violent overthrow of British rule in India. He declared himself Head of State of Free India and Commander-in-Chief of the INA.

After the war the INA was hailed by both the Congress and Muslim League as a symbol of national patriotism. From the British point of view the officers and soldiers who had joined the INA had been disloyal and should be punished. These men had engaged in 'waging war against the King–Emperor'. Of course the men claimed that they were being loyal to their own country by fighting for its independence. This conflict of ideas was exacerbated by the trials which the authorities decided to hold. To ignore the whole issue and grant an amnesty to the entire personnel of the INA would have been unjust and would have undermined morale in the Armed Forces. Eventually it was agreed that only the leaders and those charged with atrocities would be tried and there would be no attempt to punish the rank and file. Trials began in the Red Fort at Delhi, an unfortunate choice since this former palace of the Mughals had been the scene of India's former glory. The politicians opposed the trials. The first three officers to be tried were sentenced to transportation for life (the only alternative sentence to the death penalty for waging war against the King–Emperor). However, making them martyrs led to the remission of the sentence and the eventual dropping of the charge. The only charges which remained were murder and brutality.

It was in this climate that I was sent to Bala Nakamatti to face trial. In the prison camp there was also a Sikh colonel who had defected with his whole regiment to the Japanese side. I remember how incensed he was when I told him that I did not know why I was charged. A week later my papers arrived. There were three charges:

> 1. That on a certain day at a certain time, Flying Officer Chaudhry (i.e. myself) had been caught selling rations to a Bengali, and before Gokal, the Unit guard, could blow his whistle, he had shot and wounded him with a revolver.
> 2. That Flying Officer Chaudhry and Corporal Izhaq had greeted and garlanded Mr. Gandhi while they were wearing government uniform.
> 3. That Flying Officer Chaudhry and Sergeant Aslam had been heard addressing a political meeting of Mr. Jinnah's and their address had contained an incitement to revolt.

There was some truth in the first two indictments. During the Bengal famine I did give rice to our unit tailor to give to his family. Our Hindu watchman had seen me and he accused me of selling the rice. He was about to blow his whistle and summon help so I fired at his hand. He did report me and I was taken to the security police. As a result I spent the whole night in prison. During that awful night I could not sleep because of the mosquitoes. I called the guard and asked for a blanket but he refused saying I was not at home! My conscience was clear. I knew I was not guilty. It was only Gokal getting his revenge because on an earlier occasion I had refused to give him the twenty tins of milk he had demanded. It was a hot night and the mosquitoes were all over me. I threatened the guard. 'If you do not give me a blanket, when I get out, I will break your head.' He became scared and brought me a blanket to relieve me of my misery. This was all that happened over the rations issue. I could not be accused of brutality. It was only my compassion for the hungry which led me to take stores of food that would otherwise have rotted, and give them to the poor and starving.

I could not be said to be guilty where the second charge was concerned either. As our unit was connected with the intelligence service, we knew when Mahatma Gandhi and Mohammed Ali Jinnah, leader of the Muslim League were going to land on our airfields. We did garland them but this was merely out of respect. I still regard the Mahatma as the greatest political leader ever although I am well aware that there were many others who sacrificed a great deal for their country. Like all other Indians I had tremendous respect for him and believed passionately that India should be free. We did wear our uniforms on these occasions to avoid being taken and checked. It was not that we were defying regulations and asserting our political feelings.

The third charge was much more serious. I did share Subhas Chandra Bose's ideas and aspirations. Any opportunity to free India ought to be seized. If this could be achieved with Japanese help then I saw no reason why I should not support the movement.

But as an officer I had strict orders not to participate in any political activity. I was a loyal officer and believed strongly in obedience. There is no denying that Sergeant Aslam and I took part in that meeting but we were on duty and had to submit a full report of the proceedings in writing. This was a decision that had been taken that very day at the Chittagong Air Force Club. So you see, the last accusation was totally unfounded. I could not incite anyone to violence.

The Presiding Officer in charge of the camp read all the papers and returned them. No charges could be proved against me. Instead of sending me back to Chittagong he sent me to a group near Barrackpur. Although all further proceedings against the Indian National Army were dropped in April 1946, the Resolution demanding the release of all the prisoners was not carried through. I was eventually released in March, 1947.

I now seemed to be standing at the crossroads. A big question loomed up before me and a decision had to be made. What should I do with my life? There seemed no purpose at all in remaining in the Air Force. I was already deeply disenchanted with life in the Air Force. The whole business of war and fighting sickened me. With my injury I could only be offered light work. All the training in aviation and Intelligence seemed to be of no use to me now. When I began the murderous game in the Forces I was simply following my father's footsteps. I had hoped to enjoy the sights of different countries and gain a medal for meritorious service in my own right. The first I enjoyed in only a limited way in Burma and Singapore but the latter eluded me. Although I would not admit it I was perhaps haunted by that other world I had fleetingly glimpsed. Life in the Air Force with all its discrimination and prejudice seemed intolerable to me. I must get out.

Once again my family began to exert pressure upon my life. I had kept in touch with them during the time I was in the Air Force. If ever there was an illness in the family I always went. Now they demanded urgently and persistently that I return home. My mother even went so far as to initiate a private correspondence with the department about me. Because my father had died, I decided, a little reluctantly, to give in to their requests. I put forward my name for discharge.

At first it seemed that I could not go immediately. Regulations stipulated that a person in Intelligence work should be kept on in the forces for a full eighteen months commencing from the day the request for a discharge was made, but without active duty. The purpose of this was that he would forget all the secret codes and would not be able to use any information he had acquired when he returned to civilian life. I was spared this, however. Group Captain Dr. Abdullah came to my rescue. He dispensed with this condition in my case, saying that the petitioner needed immediate medical attention. I was discharged.

And so I went home. But the only thing I received in the way of 'Service Award' was the discharge papers bearing Dr. Abdullah's remarks in red ink because I had lost the sight of one eye! My mother was shocked. Her son had been given no decorations!

4: Freedom Fighter

I returned to Jammu in Kashmir in March 1947 with a sense of a great vacuum in my life. But the climate of hostility and disruption of daily life forced me to concern myself with the safety of my family and to help them in whatever way I could in the troubled times in which we were now living. Here at least was an opportunity to try and heal the breach in our relationship.

It was a very tense time for all of us. We had to be very careful in what we said and did. Hindus were in a majority in Jammu although in northern Kashmir, Muslims were in a majority. We were, therefore, conscious that we were surrounded by a hostile people. The position of Kashmir was not finally settled.

British rule in India ended in the middle of August 1947 but there were two separate countries instead of one. The Muslim country of Pakistan, with one wing in the East and the other in the West of India, was partitioned off from the rest of the country. A massive upheaval of population now took place as thousands of families uprooted themselves and trekked to the country of their choice. For Muslims this often involved a journey of several hundred miles to West Pakistan. The suffering was immense. Riots now gave place to widespread massacre. Independent states like Kashmir were given the option of acceding to whichever country they wished. However, Kashmir was one of the few important states which had not signed the Instrument of Accession which all the independent states had been invited to sign. The Maharajah of Kashmir was entangled in his own dilemma. Hari Singh, the hereditary Maharajah was a staunch Hindu. But it seems that there was intense hostility between him and Pandit Nehru, the Prime Minister of independent India. Fear that India would impose democracy in his state led him to postpone accession as long as possible. Although he had been repeatedly urged by all the political authorities to ascertain the will of the people he showed no intention of doing so. The majority of his people were Muslims. For a Hindu ruler to submit to Muslim supremacy was for him unthinkable. It is possible that he believed he could set up an independent secular state or perhaps he thought that by playing off one state against the other, he would get the best terms. Whatever his reasons he played the game of procrastination with great relish.

Meanwhile, the killings and brutalities which had begun after partition went on unabated. No one was safe anywhere. Events were moving so fast. The reign of terror was spreading and permeating every level of society. I soon discovered, however, that even in this darkness there were some little lights still shining. Not everyone is transformed into an enemy simply because the political situation changes. Our next-door neighbour, a Sikh, Iqbal Singh, a very kind and dear man, entreated us to leave the town as the situation was getting desperate. He said to me, 'If anyone threatened your lives, as your neighbours we should be obliged to defend you even with our own lives.' Such generosity of spirit and love in a sea of hatred was certainly a beacon of light in the stormy seas which threatened to drown us all. We all knew that although the majority of the people in Kashmir were Muslims that the Maharajah would eventually accede to India. There was no doubt that our lives were in constant danger. We had to do something. With great difficulty I persuaded my brothers to send their wives and children to our village home. They did this reluctantly but they could see that they had no other choice. The situation grew worse. Daily we heard news of the atrocities being committed. For example, a Muslim wrestler was murdered in broad daylight. Every restraint upon people's murderous instincts seemed to have been removed. The authorities appeared helpless to stop them. In the end I had to force my two elder brothers to leave and join their wives. This was such a heavy blow for them. Here in Jammu they had land and property. To leave would mean abandoning all they had worked so hard for all their lives. But when your life is in danger, priorities are revealed. They realised that they could not exchange their lives for their property. So, very distressed and broken, they left. I promised to stay on and look after our interests.

Soon after they left, we heard news of yet another brutal murder. A sturdy young milk and yogurt seller was stabbed to death in the Urdu market. Eventually, the terror crept nearer to us, and invaded our own factory. We had a fourteen-year-old labourer in our factory. His name was Illyas. When he didn't turn up for lunch at home one day, his younger sister came to the factory to ask what had happened to him. I told her that he did not come to work that morning but she insisted that he had left home for work as usual. My suspicions were aroused. Could he have become the latest victim? I became alarmed and feared the worst had happened. Taking the little girl by the hand we walked through the streets looking for her brother. Suddenly, to our horror, we saw him, lying dead in the gutter. I felt sick. The little one beside me who was probably only eight or nine years old began to cry uncontrollably. I tried in vain to comfort her. I had to break the news to the family. I helped to make the arrangements for his funeral and Illyas was buried the same day.

Who was going to be next on the list? We were all prime targets. Concerned as he was for our safety, our Sikh neighbour again pleaded with me to leave. It was not easy to persuade the workers to go, however, since this was their only source of income. To leave meant unemployment and consequent starvation for themselves and their families. They were also very loyal and would not entertain the thought of leaving me alone in this dangerous and difficult situation. I insisted they go and paid them all off. Sialkot, the city over the border in Punjab, Pakistan, offered some measure of safety and to it they went. I closed the factory. This was such a sad occasion for me. Our last hope to save what we had, was gone. In Jammu we had three big houses, a shop, a factory and four hundred acres of valuable land. Now all this had to be left behind. It was a costly price to pay for our new state. The idealistic concept of a separate state for Muslims—Pakistan—had triumphed. The practical problems and suffering had to be endured for the sake of it. For a noble ideal you can prepare yourself to die but was the creation of Pakistan a noble ideal? Caught up as we were in the suffering of partition, we were not so sure.

At the end of September 1947 I put on my RAF uniform, took up my gun and began walking through the street. I assumed an official manner so that I would not be molested. It was quite dark when I reached the river. The darkness provided a useful cover for me as I swam single handed across the Tui river. At the checkpoint on the other side I became alarmed and frightened when I heard the word 'halt'. The guard had seen me but noticing my officer's uniform, he said, 'Okay, I was only checking'. I continued walking. As soon as I was out of sight I ran the rest of the twenty miles to my home in Zaffarawal. My mother welcomed me with tears in her eyes. The life we had all built together had crumbled around us. What did the future hold? According to idealistic politicians it should have been an exciting and new beginning for us. We were fortunate. Our own situation was not as bleak as it could have been. We still had a comfortable house in which to live, and sufficient food. We were spared the indignity of being sent to a refugee camp.

Personally, life seemed to have lost all meaning for me. Everything seemed so pointless and empty. I was plunged into despair and depression. But I could not get rid of the idea that life did have a meaning and a purpose. It was I who had lost it and it was my job to find it again. I turned to religion to find solace and a new meaning and direction for my life. Something to live for, even to die for. My whole being craved for some purposeful activity. I was convinced that all that I was, had been trained for, and had experienced, must find a new outlet.

So I began to take Islam seriously. After all it was the religion I had been brought up in. Since it is not in my nature to do anything by half measures, I was determined to be a good Muslim. Prayer became a regular feature of my life. Muslims are obliged to pray five times a day at specific times. But I did not feel restricted by this requirement and regarded it as the minimum only. I also sought out religious teachers whom I hoped would point me in the right direction.

The way did come. The call to prepare for Holy War was being sounded from every mosque. As we had feared, the Maharajah of Kashmir had finally acceded to India. Kashmir had now become a part of India. Most Muslims were incensed. If Kashmir was not to be a part of Pakistan it ought to be independent. They were now called upon to fight for Kashmir. To fight for its independence was to fight a Holy War. This was a supreme service. The principle of 'Jihad' or 'Holy War' was regarded as a duty for all faithful Muslims if undertaken against infidels or unbelievers. Because of the essentially political nature of Islam, politics and religion have been linked together from the very beginning of its existence. Since it was my highest and supreme duty to please Allah there was only one thing for me to do —to become a freedom fighter. So began that historic period in my life when, in retrospect, I sunk to the lowest depths, when all the values my child-hood upbringing had inculcated in me seemed threatened. Yet in the darkness which shrouded my mind, I could not see this. My zeal outstripped the voice of conscience, and I succumbed to the thirst for vengeance and death. I began preparation in earnest for this new movement which seemed to offer me all I needed at this time. At last the vacuum was going to be filled. By chance, (or should I say, by the will of Allah) I met Sardar Mohammed Ibrahim, the first President of free Kashmir, who gave me his personal card and sent me to the headquarters of the Muslim army of freedom fighters.

I enlisted as a freedom fighter and joined as an ordinary soldier. I didn't want to impress anyone with my previous experience so I said nothing about my life and training in the RAF. Most of the freedom fighters were ex-army or air force men. The freedom movement was not well organised. No one was paid. The people who supported us fed us. We had no resources of our own. When nothing was available we simply killed an animal to satisfy our hunger. There were often clashes with the Pakistan National Army which would have preferred to see us as a well organised and disciplined set of fighters. In the nature of the case however, this was impossible. Our operations were short and sharp.

By October large numbers of tribesmen from the North West Frontier were pouring into Kashmir. Some of my companions and I joined them in the first attack launched from Muzaffarabad on Bada Mavla. Skirmishes on that front continued for about two months. At last as the cold grew more intense I was sent to the southern front. Here also there were several battles. The platoon I was sent to was entrusted with the specific task of blocking the road which connects Pathankot (and therefore the rest of India) with Jammu and, if possible, of seizing and occupying the road. After the Maharajah had acceded to India, Indian troops were being sent to help him in putting down riots and repelling the tribesmen. We persisted in this attempt to occupy the road although we suffered several defeats and many were killed. We did manage, however, to inflict many casualties on the opposition even while we were being beaten.

It was during the height of my involvement in the freedom movement that I met Salima again. She was delighted and was anxious to renew our friendship and even to consider marriage. My family had been stripped of their wealth and could not object now to our marrying. I too longed for this but not yet. I was too caught up in the mood of nationalist fervour and religious zeal to pursue my own happiness. We parted; but little did I know that this was to be our last meeting. Some time later I had to go to her village again. While I was there I found out that she was sick but I wasn't allowed to see her. Not knowing the extent of her illness and determined to pursue the course I had set myself, I left the village without demanding to see her. Within a month I was back in the village. It was nearly evening when I entered and the sight that greeted me sent a chill down my spine. My heart began to beat so fast that I thought my chest would burst. I saw Salima's brother and her family and relations returning from somewhere with sad faces and downcast eyes. I became alarmed and fear gripped my heart. Had anything happened to Salima? Her brother told me the worst. 'Salima died this morning. We have just buried her.' I was shattered. As I looked up I could see the sun setting. There was such a beautiful glow in the sky. The day had nearly ended. Salima's life had also been brought to a close. Did she die of a broken heart and was I to be blamed? Anguish and remorse filled me. Now the door to personal happiness was shut forever. I had lost the most precious thing I could have had. I returned to my fighting unit with a broken heart. There was only one way to drown my sorrow and that was to plunge myself even more deeply into the freedom movement. It was all I had to live for.

My commanders were not slow to see that I had had experience and training which could be invaluable to the movement. It was decided that I should become one of them and I was commissioned at a ceremony which took place at night. Everything had to be done in great secrecy in this guerilla warfare. I was made Sector Commander and was given responsibility for training the other freedom fighters. Gradually I became more and more involved in Intelligence work.

I remember one occasion vividly when we were on an operation and we had two more days to complete it. There were three of us doing Intelligence work in the hills. We ran out of food. Our diet consisted mainly of sweet corn which we used to cook in ghee. We were desperately hungry. Not far from us was the place where the Hindus burnt their dead. Hindus as you may know do not bury their dead. They are always burnt. This place was supposed to be haunted and no Hindu would loiter about there. I was never scared of anything. As I stood there wondering what to do to satisfy our hunger I had what I thought was a very good idea. I saw in the distance the smoke rising from the funeral pyre. There was a field of sweet corn nearby. I went into the field, picked some corn and made my way towards the funeral pyre. We were in enemy territory and could not light fires of our own. That would only have attracted attention to our presence. So I went and roasted the corn on the smouldering charcoal embers of the funeral pyre. My companions were pleased to see me returning with roasted corn but could not resist questioning me as to how I had managed to do it. I reluctantly told them after they had eaten. Not surprisingly, they were disgusted and began complaining of stomach pains. I was highly amused at their predictable and psychological reactions.

Our operations included all kinds of deception. On one occasion I disguised myself as a Hindu Brahmin. I had to pretend to be a Hindu refugee from Pakistan. In the uprooting of peoples after the partition of India the presence of refugees from either Pakistan or India was a common sight. I knew that I would not be conspicuous as there were thousands of Hindus in that part of India, which became Pakistan, who abandoned all their possessions and made their way into India. My mission was to find out the strength of the Indian army and its resources in that area. When I arrived at the border I began crying and related sadly how my family had all been killed and my belongings taken away. With suitable embellishment of the story, they were very impressed. They comforted me and assured me of their help. I could have a house and household things so that I could start my life all over again. I was so relieved. So far so good. But then to my dismay they asked me to recite certain Hindu mantras. These were various quotations taken from the Hindu scriptures. Now I knew quite a lot of these, having learnt them when I was at the Hindu school in Jammu. But I did not know these particular ones. The game was up. Alarmed, I had to think fast. I decided to throw myself on their mercy and began crying again. I said I was too confused and tired to recite the Mantras. Unfortunately for me they did not fall for this. They naturally became suspicious. I was becoming desperate. If they discovered who I was they would also realise that hiding in the sugar cane field nearby were some of my men. It was not difficult for them to determine whether I was a genuine Hindu or Muslim pretending to be one. I carried the mark of my true identity on my body. Like every Muslim boy circumcision had been part of my initiation rites into Islam. They only needed to strip me and examine me to discover what I was. To make matters worse I had two hand grenades hidden inside my clothes. When they took me aside to examine me I managed to wrench myself free from those who were holding me and jumped over the wall. I threw the first grenade, waited fifteen seconds and then threw the second. The whole place became engulfed in flames. My disguise thus ended in a failed mission.

Such destruction of human life and property was not in any way unusual. It was our general practice to enter a village, send everyone at the point of a gun into their houses, shut the doors securely from the outside and set the whole village alight. Somehow the inhumanity of this kind of act did not penetrate into my consciousness. I was merely doing a job and the job had to be done well. If Allah was pleased, why should I question it?

This freedom fighting went on for two whole years. At the end of these two years certain events occurred which helped to bring to the surface of my mind all those values I had learnt as a child. I could not dismiss them. The sacredness of life my mother had taught me; the desire to live for others. They had been submerged but were destined to come to the surface and to assume priority in my life again . . . Not yet, however.

As Sector Commander I found myself arranging meetings for more raids. We often received help from the Pathans from the North West Frontier who had volunteered to strengthen our numbers. They were not always of the best sort of people, more interested in women and adventures than in fighting for the freedom of Kashmir. We arranged a meeting in my sector to discuss our plans with them. As the time fixed for the meeting approached I walked through the street to the appointed place when, to my astonishment, I heard someone call my name. It was a woman's voice and sounded faint and weak. Yet I recognised it. The name she used was one that only my family and most intimate friends used. She called me 'Gama'. It was really a nickname given to me because a famous world wrestler was called by that name. When I turned and looked in the direction from which I thought the voice came I saw a young girl, the sister of some Hindu friends, standing behind a barred window. I could barely recognise her but I knew she was a member of a family my mother had sheltered in our home for two months before they could be safely taken across the border into India. I asked, 'Are you Sudesh's sister?' She nodded. 'How did you come to be here?' She was too shy and embarrassed to tell me. I pleaded with her because I could see how distressed she was. Eventually she told me of her horrible experience. Twelve Pathans had crossed the border, raided her village and brought her to this place where each one had raped her in turn. I became speechless. What was I witnessing? Is this the outcome of religious zeal? Does Islam produce this kind of behaviour? For the first time in my self-chosen career a big question mark was raised against my activities. When I saw what had happened to a family close to me, doubts began to awaken within me. This tiny spark proved difficult to extinguish. In the present situation I had to do something positive. I brought her what she wanted to soothe her pains. Then I used all my influence to get her released. I took her to my mother who kept her in the home until she was sufficiently recovered from her ordeal to cross the border and be reunited to her family.

This incident brought back to my memory a scene I had once witnessed. I was in the town of Gujarat on my way to Kashmir. As I walked through the bazaar I witnessed a sale of human beings. Unbelievable but true. The value of the three women was reflected in the prices asked for them. One woman—a virgin— was being sold for three hundred rupees; another who was married and had a small child for two hundred rupees and an old woman for fifty rupees. I remember how shocked I was. How is a human being to be valued? What is she worth? I asked myself.

5: The Unexpected Enemy

My mental equilibrium had been disturbed. I was no longer sure of myself. However, I had to go on. I could not stop in mid-stream. The pact between Pandit Nehru, the Prime Minister of India and Liaquat Ali Khan, the Prime Minister of Pakistan, was now in operation. The Indian Army benefited from this pact and strengthened its position in Kashmir. But the freedom fighters of the Free Kashmir Army began to grow demoralised. The movement and deployment of the freedom fighters were made without much forethought or planning. Almost paralysed by their limited resources these Muslim fighters were unable to fight except in stealthy night attacks.

One night I entered a village with some of my companions. The village was only a short distance inside the Indian border. I had heard that some non-Muslims still lived in the village so I summoned the Numberdar, the village headman, and asked if this was so.

'There are no Hindus, Sir,' came his reply, 'but there is one Christian household.'

'Christian? Do you mean the followers of Isa?' Isa is the Quranic name for Jesus.

'Yes; just three people.'

'Well, they are not Muslims. Come along. Take us to their house and we shall deal with them!'

This step seemed very natural to me in the light of my understanding of Christianity at this stage. I remember once asking a Maulana (a qualified teacher of Islam) for a definition of the word 'Kafir'—an infidel or unbeliever. He replied that whoever does not or is unwilling to recite the Kalimah or Muslim Creed was an infidel. The Kalimah consists of the two basic tenets of Islam: There is no god but Allah and Muhammad is the Prophet of Allah. Every true Muslim must believe and confess this basic creed. Anyone therefore who does not recite this creed is an infidel. For everyone there are just two places: the portal of peace and the portal of war. This means that unless a person accepts the creed and submits to the teaching of Muhammad he cannot have the peace and protection of Allah. He should, therefore, expect war and its consequences.

All this was straightforward and clear enough. But then I asked a specific question. What did he think about Christians? His answer threw me into confusion. He said they were also 'People of the Book'. Now Christians and Muslims both claim to worship one God and to believe the revelation He has given which is recorded in books. For the Christian these are the Old and New Testaments; for the Muslim the Holy Quran. Muslims believe moreover that the revelations given to Muhammad in the seventh century in Medina were given by the angel Gabriel and have their counterpart in Heaven. They represent God's message through all previous prophets and form God's final revelation to man. In the Holy Quran Jesus was recognised not as the Son of God but as a prophet just like all other prophets. So for Muslims the Jewish and Christian Scriptures have been replaced by the revelation given to Muhammad in the Holy Quran. Nevertheless, it seemed to me that if Christians were also 'People of the Book' they could not be in the same class as other infidels or unbelievers. But if the definition of an infidel was strictly one who did not recite the Muslim Creed, then according to his definition, they were infidels and war against them was justifiable. The Maulana would not go so far as to sanction this conclusion. Consequently, he could not approve all that my conclusion would lead me to do. This conversation had been more confusing than enlightening. I had left resolved to continue along the path I had chosen. For me the issue was clear cut. Either they were infidels or they were not. Since they did not recite the Kalimah, they were infidels and must prepare for war.

With such thoughts in my mind I set off for the house. Inside a walled rectangular courtyard which had no gate was a small room but its door was fastened from the inside. We knocked and the door was opened.

'Are you Christians?'

'Yes, we are.'

'You have been Christians up to this point. Can you not now become Muslims?'

Two middle-aged people were standing in front of me, trembling in the dim light given by an oil lamp. They were feeling round for an answer when suddenly a girl of about ten years of age crawled out from under a wooden string bed, came forward and answered my challenge.

'No, we cannot become Muslims.'

I burst out laughing, 'No one asked you. But why can't you?'

'We cannot change our religion for any reason whatever,' she replied.

'Silly girl! Nowadays you have to think about saving your life, and this is an easy way.' She did not give up easily. She continued:

'We believe in someone who said, "I am with you to the end of the world" and we believe that He is with us even today.'

It was difficult to remain patient any longer. I became irritated by her obstinacy and reached a quick decision.

'Right,' I said. 'We will make an end of the two old people, and we will take you away to camp with us and exchange you for a Muslim girl from India.' However, this little ten year old was not going to submit to my intimidation.

'Do whatever you want, but we have one request,' she persisted.

'What's that?'

'We shall not ask you to spare our lives, just give us a few minutes for prayer so that we may ask the One who gave us this promise to come to our aid,' she said confidently. No fear was in her eyes.

'Foolish girl! No god today saves anyone. No one has saved Muslims on the Indian side of the border, and no god has saved Hindus on this side. Haven't you seen the temple at Fort Haptal over there, how our demolition party razed it to the ground in a matter of hours?' I said this, trying to frighten her.

'Just let us have a few minutes,' she persisted.

'Yes, yes. You say your prayers,' I replied, and

added sarcastically, 'Just see if you can produce an atom bomb by praying.'

The girl and the two middle-aged people fell on their knees. I did not hear what they were saying in their prayer. Large tears were rolling down the girl's cheeks, and her lips were moving. Then the silence was broken with the three of them saying together, 'In the name of Jesus Christ, Amen.'

As the word 'Amen' was uttered a wall of brilliant light rose out of the ground. This wall hid the three of them from our sight. Although I had been in the habit of playing with the deathly fire and flames of high explosives I had never in all my life seen such a bright and terrifying light. It was unique, an ethereal sort of light which I am quite incapable of describing in words.

Gradually this light came closer and closer to me and I got into a panic. It seemed as if this light would advance and burn me up. I broke out in perspiration and began to dribble at the mouth. For the first time since I was nine years of age I was experiencing fear, real fear, cold fear. I did not know what to do. Suddenly the thought rose in my mind that I ought to apologise to these wretched creatures and beg their forgiveness; so I said in fear and trembling, 'Please forgive me.' Why I should have wanted their forgiveness is beyond me. They were obviously in touch with a greater power than I had ever witnessed. Perhaps I should ask 'it' for forgiveness. Anyway, I heard, 'We forgive you in the name of Jesus Christ.'

As soon as this sentence was uttered, the wall of fire vanished. They stood once more before us, peaceful and calm, ready to do whatever I commanded. We could not stay there any longer. In our possession was some jewellery we had looted from the abandoned houses of the Hindus. We threw them some of this and left. We felt as if we owed them something for the suffering we had caused.

After getting back to my quarters I could not sleep. The name of Jesus Christ kept ringing in my ears, assailing my mind again and again. I began to recall the previous experiences I had had when the name of Jesus Christ was forcefully brought to my attention. There was Baxter's 'Lord Jesus' who had protected me and my companions from the Japanese bombardment. If Baxter's claim was true, and we all acknowledged that it was the only explanation of our lives being spared, then I owed my life to Him. Yet I did not know Him personally. Furthermore, I knew little about Him. How could I show gratitude to someone I did not know? But I ought to for He saved my life.

Then there was Amber and Mary's 'Jesus Christ' in whom they had trusted and for whose sake they had saved the life of a helpless young man and looked after him. Not only had this Lord Jesus saved my life but He made sure His disciples looked after me when I was injured and helpless. Why should He do this for me? I did not give Him my allegiance. I did not know what way of life He required of His followers and was not following it. As a true Muslim I observed the law of Islam. I did not belong to Jesus Christ.

Philip Badri Nath's 'Jesus Christ' gave him strength to make great sacrifices. I too had made sacrifices. I had given up my chance for personal happiness with Salima and lost her forever because of my desire to please Allah when I responded to the call to join in the Holy War. But I did not feel a personal relationship with Allah nor believed that he gave me courage to do anything. I relied upon my own resources and ingenuity.

But most impressive of all was the little girl's 'Jesus Christ' who came and saved her at precisely the right moment. He was Someone who kept His promises. If I had any doubts about Him saving our unit during the Japanese bombardment, then I couldn't possibly have any on this occasion. I had witnessed His protection with my own eyes. There could be no escaping the fact. This 'Lord Jesus' seemed to be pursuing me wherever I went. The amazing thing is that I had asked the family to forgive me. I had never done such a thing before. Had I recognised that I was wrong to even think of murdering them? Was my whole life a sinful and wilful disobedience of doing what I innately knew to be wrong? And they had forgiven me in the name of 'Jesus Christ'.

Somehow I began to detect some pattern in all these experiences which I had. They were like scattered pearls which, when strung together, make a perfect necklace. I had been spared from certain death, cared for, shown what effect Jesus Christ's sacrificial offering could mean in people's lives and had been forgiven in His name. Was I being singled out for something? And if so, what?

Such tormenting and haunting thoughts gave me no rest. They were there and were forcing themselves upon my attention. However, they were not powerful enough as yet to drown other thoughts and commitments. I was still deeply involved in the freedom movement. I could not simply lay down my arms and walk away from it. Besides, what could I walk into? I had nothing else to which I could give myself so, although my zeal had been diminished I still carried on with my activities.

One night my platoon planned and carried out a successful night attack and set fire to a village deep inside the district of Jammu. I was standing alone in the corner of a field on the road that led into the province. I could hear the cries and shrieks of people being killed and burned in the village. I was waiting to welcome with my bullets anyone who tried to escape in that direction.

An old lady about seventy years of age came into sight through the flames, keeping the smoke and flames away from something she was carrying. She had a child about a year old flung over her shoulder. I thought it was useless to waste a bullet. A gentle blow with the butt of a revolver will be enough to finish her and the child. When I advanced towards the lady she threw the child at my feet and said:

'Kill! Go on, kill it! This is a Hindu child. Your God likes killing people, so kill it!'

My hand stopped in mid-air and I stood stock still, utterly confounded. It was one thing to kill them both without any exchanges between us and without any thought of what I was really doing. To be made aware of their presence in this direct way and to be challenged to carry out my task was more than I could take. Taking advantage of my stillness and obvious hesitation, the lady came forward and, looking me straight in the eyes, asked me boldly,

'Son, do you have any children?'

'No, mother. My brothers have.' The fact that I did not lose my sense of respect for the elderly by calling her 'mother' shows the state of my mind.

'Have you watched those children closely when they make mud houses during the rainy season?'

'Yes, mother, I myself have made mud horses, oxen and houses several times.'

This conversation was gradually disarming me. How clever she was, engaging me in conversation the way she was doing. She continued:

'And how did you like it if anyone broke down those mud houses and toys?'

'I got very annoyed, mother,' I replied rather sheepishly.

'Well then, my son. Just imagine that this little soul is a God-made body or sort of toy which His hands have made and which expresses His goodness. If you were disgusted when anyone ruined anything you had made then how can you think that God likes all these things that you are doing? Is God so weak that He asks your help in killing infidels? If God does not like any person or thing then He is well able to put an end to it Himself. Why does He tell you to kill infidels or His people?'

These words struck in my mind and soul like a sledgehammer and I shouted out:

'That's enough, mother! After today these hands will never be raised against anyone in the name of religion. You have made me realise what an utter wretch I am. I will put an end to this. Dear mother, pray for me. I know that I am lost.'

I realised deep down in my heart that she was right. She had brought to a climax all the doubts I was beginning to have concerning the movement I was in. My resolve to continue in this warfare had been considerably weakened already. Now at last I could not go on. I was completely broken. I ordered my section to withdraw for retreat. The men thought I was silly or mad and began grumbling amongst themselves. This was so unlike me they were baffled. Nevertheless, they obeyed.

That night I took stock of myself and my violent life. What I saw made me feel that everlasting punishment in hell was the only place left for a person like me because with my own hands I had ruined what belonged to God. God Almighty had brought the whole universe into being; I had destroyed the noblest creation of that same God. Still I would not accept all responsibility for what I had done. Surely I was only the means by which it was done. I merely submitted to a divine mandate as expounded by our religious teachers. But if I was not responsible for this whole game of bloodshed, who was? God?

Tormented by these thoughts I came to the conclusion that I could not go on with my present life. I no longer felt that I was pleasing Allah by killing 'kafirs'. I had to get out. Resignation was the only course open to me. Yet I could not bear to think of the consequences. I only knew that it had to be done. I went to the Commanding Officer and asked him if I could resign from the freedom movement. Amazement and disbelief were written all over his face. 'Why, why do you want to resign?' he demanded. I could not bring myself to tell him the whole story. It would seem too fantastic to him. In any case I could not explain to anyone at this stage what I was really thinking. I had not had time to work it out for myself. So I merely told him that I was not bound to the movement. I received no salary from it and they had no claim upon me. I had freely joined and now I wanted freely to resign. He realised that it was futile to go on arguing with me or trying to persuade me to stay on. He asked for my resignation in writing. This gave me a chance to put down my thoughts coherently. I wrote four pages, trying as best as I could to explain the reasons for my wanting to resign. He read these patiently and carefully. He told me in no uncertain terms what he thought of me. I had gone crazy, he said. I thanked him for his opinion and said that I was happy I had become crazy. Through this weakness in my brain, the light was penetrating. I was coming to my senses at last. The Commanding Officer was just baffled. But he offered me another job which I accepted. This was to gather together into one place all the moveable property abandoned by the Hindus when they fled across the border into India. With me were some other volunteers of the Muslim National Guard and a religious guide.

This job brought me back to my family again. One day when I arrived home for a meal my late brother Haji Khuda Bakhsh saw that I had a very beautiful scarf and asked me where I had found it. I explained that I had taken it from the confiscated property from one of the Hindu's houses. My brother took it from me and threw it on the fire. 'You have disgraced yourself and us by taking this scarf,' he exclaimed in anger. Now you will remain at home and in future, starting tomorrow, you will not go on this duty connected with plundering property! Have you heard me?'

I was amazed. It was not that I was doing anything extraordinary. Even our religious teachers did not consider it beneath them or immoral to take and use abandoned property. I remember a certain Maulvi who had taken earthenware ovens belonging to Hindus and placed them in his own home. This man was well known to our family. When he was away at Deoband and Bulandshahr, two training colleges for Muslim religious leaders in northern India, my father helped to support him financially. He even managed to appropriate a great mansion abandoned in a nearby Hindu village.

One day I had seen him claiming in the presence of a district official that he was a refugee from India! He had filled in a claim form which stated that he had left a great deal of agricultural land in India and wished to be compensated for it. How true the saying is that goes:

'I found many robbers dressed up as leaders,
Should I save myself or my honour?'

Yet here was my brother, filled with rage over my taking a simple handkerchief. Whose example could I trust? Here I was again in confusion and disillusionment and with no job to do. What was I to do with my life?

6: Closed in and Conquered

My confrontation with the old lady on that fateful night had wrenched from me the vow never to take another human life. In my determination to keep that vow I had resigned from the freedom movement. After I left the RAF, the desire to please Allah had led me into the movement to fight for a free Kashmir. My life once again seemed to have meaning and purpose. But now neither my religious zeal nor my political enthusiasm fired my imagination. Instead I was appalled at the brutalities and atrocities of war of any kind, and for whatever purpose. So once more I was stopped, as it were, in my tracks. I was standing at a crossroads and did not know which way to take.

Instead of emptiness, however, I was filled with doubts and fears. One fear in particular would not leave me: the fear of dying and going to hell. I could not see any other destiny for myself. Death seemed so real to me. I wondered what would become of me if I died then. I, who had rarely experienced fear since I was nine years old and who was never afraid of dangerous missions and had often come near to death, was now caught in the iron grip of fear; fear of what I knew I deserved. Yes, I saw myself fit only for hell.

Then doubts would assail me and throw me into even greater confusion. What if there was no God? I could not then be punished for what I had been and what I had done. There was no need to fear hell. I had seen death and wanton destruction of human life all around me. God could not possibly have been in all this. But the voice of conscience refused to be silenced. Back it would come with authority and conviction: 'There *is* a God'. The very existence of the universe was proof enough to me that someone was the source of its origin and is its architect. If this was not so then God was not closely involved with his creation and the world would be desolate and unattractive. But I knew this was not the case. The beauty of nature was and is inescapable.

Even if I conceded that there was a God who had created this world and all its beauty, why did He allow destruction of what He himself had made? I sincerely believed, and was encouraged by our religious leaders to think, that Allah was pleased when infidels or unbelievers were killed. How could this be if He had created all men? Surely, a better way would be to win their allegiance?

Perhaps God himself was not responsible for the misuse man makes of his free will and was displeased with the killing of human beings rather than approving. But God must ultimately be responsible, I thought, since it was He who gave man free will in the first place. When I killed infidels I felt I was given a divine mandate to do so. If God was displeased then He could easily have overruled my will to accomplish his own ends. As a devout Muslim I believed that I had acted correctly in responding positively to the call from the mosque to engage in

Holy War. I had submitted. Islam after all means 'submission'. I could not therefore be held responsible for all I had done. If I were not responsible then there was no need to feel guilty and to deserve hell. Since I was not guilty there was no reason to repent. No repentance, no forgiveness and no reconciliation. Maybe I was totally wrong. Perhaps I should have exercised my free will in such a way that I did not do things which my own conscience condemned. And if my conscience condemned me, if there is a God, He must surely be greater than my conscience.

The more I thought about these things the more confused and despairing I became. My mind was torn and racked by these tormenting thoughts. I felt like a man who has been utterly misled. There was not a glimmer of light left in my life. I was ill-equipped mentally to cope with such questions. My state of mind was such that I could not sleep at night. Sometimes I would lie awake thinking and only dropping off to sleep from sheer mental exhaustion. Maybe I should give up trying to find an answer, I told myself. Perhaps all religions were man-made fabrications by people who wanted to make ordinary people feel inadequate. It was futile to distress myself like this.

But my tormented mind could not easily find solace in this refuge. Questions kept going round and round in my mind. I could not silence them. There had to be an answer. I had to find it. I began getting up early in the morning but this only increased my problems. The questions demanded answers and I had found none. Sleep and food meant nothing to me. Once I went without food for seventeen days and nights.

This inner turmoil was aggravated by my own behaviour and attitude and of those around me. I had become very irritable and difficult to get on with. My company was no longer wanted by my friends and they began to avoid me. I ran down all religion and was highly contemptuous of its values. I totally rejected any counselling from our Muslim religious leaders. People began to say that I had probably gone mad. They surmised that the many killings I had been involved in had disturbed my mind. I must be mentally unbalanced, they were saying. I did not know whether it was I who disliked people or whether people disliked me. Perhaps it was mutual.

I even became estranged from my own family. I knew that I was a stranger in our home and none of the family liked to talk to me. They could not understand what was happening to me and felt quite helpless. There seemed to be nothing they could do to help me. Despair of this kind can often turn very easily into resentment. My poor mother was greatly distressed by all this.

'Tell me, my son, what your difficulty is and I will help you,' she implored. But no one could help me. I was wretched because of the misery I was causing and yet I could do nothing about it. I seemed locked in an ever-decreasing spiral of disturbing thoughts and demanding questions.

Just occasionally and very fleetingly, a little shaft of light would penetrate the enclosing darkness and the thought would occur to me that not all of life was empty and meaningless. There was a God. The impressive regularity of the world speaks eloquently of a controlling power. To this power the whole world, man and the rest of creation, must somehow be accountable. Man cannot be free to do whatever he likes without any thought of the consequences of his actions. Neither has he been put into a world of random forces and subject to whatever fate these decreed. I became increasingly determined to find this power or God and make my peace with Him. I too was beginning to fear for my sanity if I did not find this peace. I realised I could not find it where I was. It had proved too elusive. I was isolated from those who loved me and whom I loved.

At the beginning of May 1949 I quietly left home. I had no idea where I was going. I had one burning desire—to find peace. I did not say goodbye to my family. Regrettably, I never saw the need for this.

My search began in earnest. Where should I begin? On reflection it seems strange to me that I did not turn to Christianity. I had seen people in whom the peace I was seeking was visibly present. Yet I made no effort to look in that direction. I was still a Muslim and so I determined to examine Islam more carefully before I discarded it. A man may renounce a lot of things in life but to renounce his religion without very strong reasons seems folly to me. When that religion is Islam it becomes even more difficult. For Islam involves a total commitment of one's whole life to Allah. I had no serious doubts or hesitation in accepting the first part of its basic tenet: 'There is no god but Allah'. For me there could be only one God. This Islam gloriously proclaimed. Just how remarkable this belief is can be seen when one looks at the religious Arabic background from which Islam sprang. The Arabs were polytheistic and idolatrous. It is believed that there were 360 idols in the Ka'aba, a shrine in Mecca revered by the Arabs because of the black meterorite stone embedded in one of its walls. The cult of the goddesses Lät, Mānat, and Uzza was a firmly established part of the religion. These were known as the daughters of Allah. Allah was the supreme deity. It was this latter notion that Mohammed turned into the dominant belief of Islam as he abandoned the polytheism. To embrace this belief was to embrace a noble truth. Yet Islam had already become discredited in my eyes. Could it possibly give me what I wanted?

According to our religious leaders, Allah commands his followers to engage in Jihad or Holy War against infidels. It was involvement in the Holy War which had brought me into the state of despair I was now in. I did not give up easily, however. I delved deeper and found that Islam also teaches that if I perform good deeds now I could hope for forgiveness in life after death. But what I wanted was forgiveness now, and peace and reconciliation in this life. After my death it would be too late. To live the rest of my life just hoping to be forgiven after death was not enough to satisfy me and rescue me from my present predicament. In addition I found it difficult to respect and listen to our Maulvis. I recalled the words of my father: 'Listen, my son, the majority of the Maulvis are immoral people. Listen to what they say but do not follow their example. They send innocent people to the gallows in the same way as they killed the mystic Mansoor. Certainly, respect them but do not trust them. And if it is possible keep them well away from your home.'

My father probably said this at a time when a woman was taken in questionable circumstances from the house of a certain gentleman who was able to recite the whole of the Arabic Quran by heart. It is the ambition of religious Muslims that by the age of twelve their sons should be able to recite the whole of the Arabic Quran and so become Hafiz e Quran—a Protector of the Quran. The fact that this Maulvi was a Hafiz e Quran did not prevent him from indulging in immoral practices. It was as a direct result of the impure lives of the religious leaders that my father stopped going to the Mosque to join in the corporate prayers which Muslims are accustomed to do on Fridays at midday in order to preserve their corporate identity.

The mystic Mansoor, to whom my father referred and whom he greatly admired, lived in the tenth century. He was put to death in a barbarous way at Baghdad. To orthodox Muslims he was a blasphemous heretic. He had uttered in two words the sentence *'Anna Haqq'*—*'I am God'*. It was a doctrine of personal deification. He had achieved the ultimate in mysticism—perfect union with the diety. But any blurring of the distinction between God, the ultimate reality, and man His created being, could not be acceptable to orthodox Muslims. My father, who regarded himself as a mystic, probably never saw this difficulty. For him the words of a Persian verse,

> *'Men of God never wholly become God,*
> *But they are never separate from God either.'*

expresses more truly his understanding of the relationship between God and man.

As I reflected upon my father's words and ideas, it struck me that like him, I too could become a mystic.

Maybe here I could find the peace I was seeking. As I have mentioned earlier, in the Islamic world of the eighth or ninth century men of devotion who sought the peace of a contemplative life were called mystics or sufis. In many ways they resembled the Christian hermits who flourished in the Middle East. For them the obedience demanded by Islam to an external code of human behaviour was secondary. The primary thing was worshipful response of the human heart to a God of love. They believed in direct experience of God. Surely, I thought, this was what I desired above all else.

It was becoming obvious to me that I needed help. My lonely search was getting me nowhere. Consequently, I spent many a wakeful night at various shrines and cultivated the company of many 'holy men'. However, the more I sought the company of 'holy' and 'godly' men, the more disappointed I became. Perhaps this was in part due to my military training which made me sceptical, and made it difficult for me to believe anyone easily. Whenever I considered the life of these men carefully, I discovered that although they claimed to be searchers for divine truth, they were always shown to be misled and sadly misguided. I found them involved in such horrific activities that I am ashamed to relate them. When, in turn, I considered the hereditary spiritual leaders, the pirs, I was pained to see their way of life. While their peasant labour went hungry, they were engaged in such frivolous pastimes as importing dogs from Russia for breeding purposes. Those labouring in the fields belonging to these pirs could not feed their children, but the precious dogs were being fed fresh meat twice a day.

The contemplation of such decadence reduced me to a state of mental paralysis.

I did not give up easily, however. I went so far as to join a group of Muslim students who indulged in the use of drugs, music and dance to induce the mystical state of consciousness of God. Yet this proved a futile exercise and I gained nothing. Instead I grew worse. My search for peace had ended in complete disillusionment. In my despair I recalled the opening words of the Quran:

> *'Guide us on the right path,*
> *The path of those upon whom Thou hast*
> *   bestowed thy favours*
> *Not upon those upon whom wrath is brought down*
> *Nor those who go astray.'*

The 'right path' is generally taken to mean the Muslim Faith. 'Sirat'—the word for 'Way' is also the name of a very narrow bridge across the mouth of hell over which only good Muslims will be taken safely; others will fall into hell.

Having lost all confidence in man-made creeds I felt nevertheless that there must be a way of escape and asked God to show me the way in this life and the way of deliverance from my own hell. I had continued to get up early in the morning but instead of it being a time of questioning I began earnestly to pray and to ask God or rather to implore him to guide me. From the inner depths of my being my cry for spiritual help went up:

> 'O Lord Almighty! It is impossible to deny your Being. Every vein and fibre of my being is a

85

manifestation of your glory. The whole of creation is a locus of your being. I acknowledge your existence. My soul affirms your being. I acknowledge also that you have created me and all men. I am conscious that by imitating worthless religious leaders and by acting on their destructive counsel, I have oppressed those created by you. My evil deeds convince me that hell is my portion, for you, O Master, will judge sinners. I do not trust any religions and creeds in this world. O my Lord, show me the straight path. I do not want to go to hell. If you exist, show me the right path so that I may behold you. I am suffering, O Master. I desire peace of mind and cannot find it. Help me, Lord. My consciousness of my sin pierces me like a lancet. Have mercy on me, O God, have mercy, Amen.'

I do not remember the date but it was three or four o'clock in the morning and I was making my usual supplications. I was weeping bitterly and was more than usually despondent. I was in the waiting room of a railway station when this particular prayer was uttered. Suddenly I was conscious that someone had come up behind me, put a loving hand on my shoulder and said, 'My grace is sufficient for you!' This sentence was repeated three times and when it was repeated the third time, I felt as if an electric charge had gone through my body and the weight on my mind was immediately lifted. It was as if an invigorating and exhilarating ecstasy had unexpectedly overtaken me. I felt lifted up and experienced what I can only describe as a union with God. Nothing seemed to separate us. The sense of forgiveness and reconciliation was so real. I began rapturously repeating the sentence, 'My grace is sufficient for you'. I had never experienced such depth of happiness and joy before. It was truly 'heavenly'.

A railway employee was cleaning near the bench where I was lying and when he saw my state he stopped and asked, 'Son, are you a Christian?' When I shook my head, he was amazed and said, 'Then why do you keep repeating these words, "My grace is sufficient for you"?' I replied, 'I do not know why I am repeating these words. All I know is that someone has just said them to me and he also showed me some tablets with all my evil deeds written on them. But with one sweep of his hand he wiped all these tablets perfectly clean. Since that moment I have felt like a new man. The entire burden has been lifted from my spirit. My heart wants to sing aloud.'

'It is the Lord you must thank, my son, for this deliverance,' he told me. 'The one who came to you was the Lord Jesus Christ. He said these words to the apostle Paul. I do not remember exactly where but I know that it is written in the sacred New Testament. The Lord Jesus now wants you to become His servant.'

'How sir? How can I become His servant?'

'Be baptised in the name of the Lord Christ, and begin to follow Him at once.'

'Tell me exactly what I must do, sir. I have reached the turning point of my life.'

'My son, I know nothing more. I only know that if you go from here to Tandlian-wala and then on to

Isanagri there is a clergyman there called the Rev. Inayat Rumal Shah. He will help you.'

This old man now put down his broom and came even closer to me, his eyes filled with tears. I embraced him, clasping him firmly in my arms. We both cried freely and gave vent to our deepest emotions. For a brief moment I wondered if he might be the father of that little girl whom I and my companions had gone to murder. I couldn't bear that thought. He could not be or I should surely have recognised him! How deeply moved I was that this man who obviously belonged to that dispised and lowest of all classes, the sweepers, should have been there to show me the next step. It is not difficult to see why so many among their class accept the gospel of Jesus Christ. In Him they find their true selves. Realising that they are made in God's image, that they are his children, they find new dignity and worth. I was happy to be identified with them.

With the words, 'My grace is sufficient for you' resounding in my ears, and my heart full of joy, I got on the train for Isanagri. The turmoil had at long last ended. Now peace reigned. Oh! What bliss it was. It almost overwhelmed me. My mind could not take it all in. The Lord Jesus Christ who had saved me from physical death, had cared for me in my illness, had shown me his sacrifice and had revealed to me his all-sufficient grace, had now conquered my heart. He had triumphed. No more would I wander aimlessly about the world, seeking a purpose and meaning which kept eluding me. I found the real meaning and purpose for my life. I had found Him who gives us his peace and reconciles us to Himself. He is mine and I am His.

7: Beginning of Pilgrimage

I had been wonderfully freed from the hopeless despair which had darkened my heart and mind. My heart was overflowing with joy as I got off the train at Isanagri village in Faisalabad District, and met the Rev. Inayat Rumal Shah. He greeted me very warmly and offered me hospitality. After our meal he smiled gently at me and asked, 'Well sir, why do you want to become a Christian?' Not knowing anything of my background or my deep longing for peace which had been satisfied so miraculously earlier, he seemed almost casual as if that was the most normal question to ask. But I was not choosing Christ or Christianity. It was not a question of my wanting to become a Christian. Jesus Christ had chosen me himself. Not wanting to upset the Padre, I answered simply, 'Somebody told me to, about three or four o'clock this morning Jesus Christ himself met me and said, "My grace is sufficient for you".' There was a picture of Jesus Christ crucified on the wall. Mr. Rumal Shah took hold of my hand and with the other hand he pointed to the picture. Is it the same Jesus Christ who had spoken to me I wondered? I heard Mr. Rumal Shah saying, 'People robbed Christ even of his own clothes! He is a helpless person! What will

He give you?' The implication of that question might have upset me if I were in a different frame of mind. I did not want anything except His peace. Salvation was what I sought and had found. If I were a conceited person I might have become angry and upset. I might have thought that I should have been welcomed with open arms. But the whole situation was still too new and too overwhelming for me. These emotions found no place in my heart which was so full of happiness.

Of course I did not know then but I soon found out that enquirers or those seeking to become Christians are nearly always regarded initially with great suspicion. It would seem that many want to become Christians because they are attracted by some of the benefits which the missionaries offer. A good education, or even more basic things like food, clothes, and shelter. Not surprisingly, perhaps, is the fact that the majority of Hindus converted to Christianity have come from the 'sweeper class', the poorest of the poor. One must not assume however, that all these converts have come for material gain. Like me some, or even the majority, must have found in Christianity the satisfaction of their deepest longings and for them the words:

> *'Nothing in my hand I bring,*
> *Simply to thy cross I cling,*
> *Wash me Saviour or I die.'*

must have a ring of truth.

To Padre Sahib's question I could only reply, 'Do not say that Christ is helpless and can offer me nothing. He has already given me everything. He has made me a new man and has given me peace of mind.'

'Good,' he said, 'The only thing I can do for you is to send you to a missionary friend of mine in Gojra. He will do something for you.'

There was to be no instant acceptance of me. Not that I could expect it but the road ahead was to be a long one. A few minutes later Mr. Rumal Shah put a letter in my hand and gave me some money so that I could go to Gojra by bus. What an inauspicious beginning to my pilgrimage! Still I was in no way disheartened or discouraged. My new found faith meant too much for me. I had at last found the 'pearl of great price' and nothing or no-one was going to rob me of it.

I reached Gojra in the afternoon and met the missionary, the Rev. R. W. F. Wootton. By now I think I was fully aware that the way forward was not going to be easy. Mr. Wootton told me that they would first have to test the genuineness of my decision to become a Christian and then a decision would be made about baptism. I gladly agreed. Baptism was a momentous step. It was not something that was done to one as part of the natural course of events. It meant a deliberate commitment to Christ and the gospel of the kingdom of God. A whole new life style and set of values opened up before the convert. Inevitably, in a country with a non-Christian history, it does involve uprooting and a crossing of ethnic barriers. For some it can become a very painful experience. Baptism is never undertaken lightly. To be a Christian in an Islamic country which was consciously and deliberately created for Muslims is almost, not quite, like committing a treasonable act. Muslims who become Christian converts are relinquishing the 'privilege of living in a Muslim state as a Muslim'. I knew that in some Muslim countries converts were excluded from the protection of the law. Such people could not apply to the courts for justice when their property or persons were damaged or molested. It was not uncommon for Muslim converts to lose their lives for their faith. I was happy to be tested. In the process both they and I could ascertain the true object of my allegiance.

Mr. Wootton arranged for me to have the visitor's room in the compound. The only furniture in that room was a rickety old bed with two quilts. If I drew the quilts up, the heat bothered me; if I put the quilts off, the mosquitoes flew away bloated with my lovely red blood! No proper arrangements had been made about food for me. If I was given any I ate it; if no-one thought about it, I went hungry. On one occasion no one thought about it for three days! For the first two days I managed to survive and spent a lot of time in prayer. But by the third day I was so weak I took to my bed. Mr. Wootton had been away from the Christian compound (the name given to the area where the homes of the missionaries and staff were) and when he returned, he came into my darkened room. 'Are you ill, brother?' he asked.

'No, I am not ill, sir,' I replied faintly.

'Then why are you so weak? Have you had anything to eat?'

I shook my head and he asked, 'For how long?' There was not much strength in my body and however much I tried I could not prevent my eyes welling up with tears. I indicated with my fingers that I had not eaten for three days. He was very distressed at this news, and sat comfortingly on my bed.

'What kind of people are we?' he asked. 'How mean and cruel! I was not here, but was there not a single person living on the compound who thought about you or enquired about your meals?'

'It does not matter, sir. I thought that this might be part of my testing and so I did not mention it to anyone. I did not even go out of this room because people on the compound were whispering unkind things about me. One said that I wanted to become a Christian simply because I wanted to find a young girl to marry. Another said that I was looking for employment as a mission servant. Yet another said that I merely wanted money. I heard it all but said nothing.'

The people on the compound had been unkind to me right from the start. To them I was an intruder. This was their privileged position—to be working for the missionaries. They had no time for me, and dismissed me as just another 'bread and butter' Christian.

I was beginning to feel pity rather than hurt or anger towards these Christians. They are perhaps the saddest group of people. Living in the mission compounds, they are naturally cut off from their own people. They vie with each other to gain the missionary's acceptance and admiration and this tends to breed hypocrisy rather than sincerity. Instead of welcoming enquirers as those who are seeking a higher goal and deeper meaning for their lives, they tend to despise them and treat them as rivals. The sacrifices that enquirers may be willing to make find no kind of response from them. They seem intent on pleasing the missionaries rather than the

Master to whom they have committed their lives. I was merely a victim of this attitude.

Mr. Wootton showed me every kindness, however. 'Right,' he said, 'get up and come to my house.' When we arrived he instructed his cook, 'You are to cook meals for this man and give them to him whether I am here or not. Is that clear?'

Well, I never went without food again but the atmosphere in the compound did not change. People's attitudes never altered. In fact it became intolerable. As a result I persuaded Mr. Wootton to make arrangements for me to stay in the hostel. In the compound there was a mission school and a hostel.

During this time I did not tell Mr. Wootton anything about myself. The past did not seem important. I did not want any knowledge of my wealthy background or the fact that I had been an RAF officer to influence his treatment of me in any way. When therefore he suggested I become a night watchman or security guard I gladly accepted it because I did not wish to spend my life being a burden to anyone. The school and hostel at Gojra were closed during the month of June. Consequently, arrangements for me were entrusted to a Christian in the compound who was a very saintly man. His name was Sewak Boota Masih. I was extremely fortunate to be working alongside such a man. He was a messenger in the Girls' school and hostel. His wage was exceedingly small and yet he used to help people like myself.

> 'Fret not, this upturned world! Its generous men
>   are humble,
> Who serve the God of truth, you never hear them
>   grumble'

94

Boota Masih could only read Gurmukhi (written Punjabi, the language of the Sikhs). His friendship formed the basis of my spiritual growth. It was from him that I learnt the true nature of the Christian faith and what a practical Christian life involved. Prayer played a very important part in his life. One could almost say that his whole life was one of prayer. We used to spend whole nights together in prayer. I remember being with him one night before I went on duty. We got so caught up in prayer that time passed without our ever noticing it. To my amazement, people the next day said they had seen me four times during the night. They wondered why I had been so zealous in my duty. I then realised what a wonderful thing had happened. While we were praying, Jesus himself had done my duty! My heart rejoiced in my Saviour who was making Himself so real to me.

At the end of September 1949 I was told that my baptism would take place on the 2nd October at the first meeting of the Gojra Convention. Some questions were put before me to ascertain the depth of my understanding of the nature of the step I was taking. One of them concerned the amount of Christian literature I had read. I was delighted to be able to say that I had read nearly all Mr. Wootton's library of Urdu books plus a considerable number of his English ones.

On the night of September 30th, as I was praying, the Lord roused my conscience, pointing out to me that I had not been fully honest with Mr. Wootton. The fact that I had not told him about my past seemed to suggest that I had something to hide. This was cowardly and deceptive and was an obstacle in my spiritual growth and progress. I found it impossible to relax after this revelation. I got up there and then in the middle of the night and went to Mr. Wootton's house. I had to unburden myself and told him everything about my past. He was pleased with my frankness and honesty and we had a good time of prayer together.

My baptism took place on October 2nd and the seal of belonging to Christ, of being a 'Christian' was stamped upon me. It gave me great joy that in accepting baptism I was following the example of our Lord. I had now become a visible part of the Christian brotherhood; now these are my people and I am a member of this household. As a sign of the debt I owed to my humble friend and my appreciation of what his friendship meant to me I took as my baptismal name the name of 'Ghulam' (slave) and added 'Masih' (Messiah/Christ) so that it also expressed for me my new vocation—to become a slave of Jesus Christ.

For the next two weeks I lived in a state of great happiness. The sense of belonging to Christ and to the Christian fellowship lifted me onto another plane. My Lord was so real to me. Daily the resolution to serve Him for the rest of my life grew in strength and intensity. I truly felt God's favour resting upon me and knew what it was like to be loved by my Creator and to feel a responsive love stirring within me, unworthy as I felt myself to be.

I soon learnt, however, what it was like to be put through the refining fire. My outward circumstances suddenly changed drastically. It happened on a day when the compound seemed to be deserted. Neither Mr. Wootton, nor Master Charan Dass, head of the Boys' hostel, nor even the Rev. B. M. Augustine who baptised me was there. I learnt later that they had all gone to Lahore for a meeting. I was alone when I was confronted by an angry maternal uncle and my elder brother who had arrived that day. They had come for me.

In most Eastern countries the word 'family' almost by definition includes not only mother, father, brothers and sisters but uncles and aunts and cousins on both the maternal and paternal side. One has duties and responsibilities to all of them. Good relationships with them are important in the shaping of one's own destiny. I could not ignore them with impunity. It would have been almost impossible for me to declare my independence of them. They had wealth, power and influence. My uncle gave me two options. The first was that I should go away with them immediately and without telling anyone where I was going. The second was really a threat. If I refused to go with them they would go into the town and make the news of my conversion public. This would so anger the people that both I and all the Christians in Gojra would be mercilessly beaten up. The well being of my new Christian family was at stake if I did not do as they asked. I could not allow any harm to come to my fellow Christians. Although deeply upset and a little uncertain how I should meet this crisis so early in my Christian pilgrimage, I remembered to whom I had given my allegiance. It was my Master's bidding that I wanted to obey and no one else's. His will was to be the guiding force in my life. Therefore I said simply to my uncle, 'I will ask my Master'.

I shut the door of my room and asked the Lord what I should do. I was left in no doubt. He told me, 'There are still a lot more thorny obstacles for you to overcome as you follow me. Go with them, for there at home is the very first place where you have to begin your work of witnessing for me. You are to stand as my witness, "First in Jerusalem, then in Judea, then Samaria, and then in the whole world" '. How amazing that I should have been commissioned in the same way as the disciples were in the Acts of the Apostles.

I returned to my relatives and said that I was ready to go with them. I was not afraid to entrust myself to them for I knew at whose bidding I was doing it and I knew whose hands were underneath, upholding me. So I accompanied them to Lyallpur (now called Faisalabad).

8: Miraculous Escape

My conversion had given me peace of mind and a meaning and purpose for my life. What a transformation this was from the state I was in when I was last with my family. Unfortunately, this meant nothing to them. They had only one consuming passion: to get me to renounce Christianity and become a 'good Muslim' again. They could not ignore my existence and my new profession of faith. It was a reproach to them. People of their standing could not have a convert in the family. After all only the poorest of the poor became converts. As one of the poor Christians I would have to mix with them socially. This was disgraceful and intolerable. My family were scandalised. I remember being told by one of my nieces later that as a result of my conversion many of her suitors turned away. Who I was and what I had become had distressing repercussions for my family. I just had to be made to see the error of my ways.

Islam was for them such an exalted and noble religion. How could I possibly exchange it for Christianity? There is only one true God and Muhammad was his prophet—that was what had been drummed into every Muslim child from his earliest years. But here I was declaring that Jesus Christ was not simply a prophet like the other prohets including Moses and Abraham, but the Son of God. That was blasphemy and was anathema. God did not have sons! Since the Muslim conception of sonship was purely physical, this confession was the ultimate blasphemy. And yet, the metaphorical use of the concept of sonship was not foreign to Islamic tradition. One of Muhammad's great friends was called Abu Harera, 'Father of Cats'. He was so fond of these little animals that he never went anywhere without one, sometimes hiding an animal in his garments. Such was his love for them. Another one of Muhammad's uncles who did not accept him as a prophet was called Abu Jehal, 'Father of Ignorance'. In other words 'sonship' or 'fatherhood' could be used of relationships which were totally removed from a physical relationship. Sometimes people dismiss as nonsense something they cannot face; the challenge can be too much. It can wipe out the very foundation of one's position. If a Muslim were to accept Jesus as the Son of God then the significance of Muhammad as Allah's prophet and his revelation must necessarily take second place to the one who is God's Son and has given God's fullest revelation to mankind.

Muslims also believe that good works done in this life will gain for them forgiveness for their sins and happiness in the next life. I, on the other hand, saw the need for the forgiveness of my sins now so that I could give my life to God and let Him determine the nature and course of my life now. To my family I had become a kafir—an unbeliever. They did not hesitate to treat me as such. On my return to my home, I was compelled to eat my meals in the street. Nevertheless, I gave thanks and ate without murmur. Their persecution gave me an opportunity to witness publicly to my Lord.

No stone was left unturned to bring me back to the fold. My uncle took me to his village in Sheikhupura District. Religious teachers were sought out and brought to the house to try and reason with me. One newly trained Maulvi (a religious teacher) gave up after a short while and in desperation issued a certificate of insanity before he left. If I were going to be so obstinate, then I could at least be dismissed as mad.

Six weeks of meetings with various Maulvi proved to be of no avail. It was then finally decided that I should meet Sayyed Ata Ullah, Shah Bakhari (a descendant of the Prophet Muhammad) who was to visit Sheikhupura about that time. At the appointed hour I was ushered into Shah Sahib's presence, but instead of conversing with me and trying to get me to renounce Christianity, he laughed loudly and derisively and said,

'So you have become a Christian?'

'Yes,' I replied. There was an uneasy silence. 'Please go on and say more, Shah Sahib', I said, the tone of my voice expressing both respect and annoyance.

'What more can I say?' the Shah Sahib said contemptuously.

'A little more advice and guidance perhaps', I answered, being curious to see what he had to say to someone in my position who might be willing to renounce his faith if persuaded to do so.

'What kind of guidance do you want? There is

only one reason for which people like you become Christians.'

I knew what he was thinking. He was attributing my conversion to a desire to marry a Christian girl. I could restrain my anger no longer. I asked permission to speak and replied: 'Shah Sahib, I have come to listen to you because my family has great hopes that you would set me on the 'Right Way' but I did not expect such coarse imputations from you. What is more, I should like to say that sex and religion are two different things altogether and anyone who rejects or accepts a religion for reasons of sex is a fool. I would also like to point out that as a Muslim I was entitled to four wives, more if I could manage it! After my death I could hope for seventy-two houris (wives) in paradise. But Shah Sahib, religion and faith transcend such earthly considerations. They cannot be compromised just for sex. You have accused me of allowing sex and marriage to be the foundation of my new faith and yet, by all accounts, I could have a better prospect in both of these if I were to become a Muslim again. Your arguments are contradictory.'

My outburst caused the Shah Sahib to lose all control and he roared in anger: 'Be quiet you ill-mannered lout!'

I meekly said, 'Shah Sahib, there is no need for anger; let us reason together.'

'Throw him down the stairs! The cheek!' shouted the Shah. My brother's feelings were at last aroused. 'I forbid you to lay a finger on him. If it had been simply a matter of beating him up, the family would have done it', my brother retorted. All three of us came downstairs.

After these totally unsuccessful efforts my brother and uncle began to realise that I could not be easily persuaded to abandon my new faith. They decided to send me to Lahore. My uncle's relative, Hussain Ali, probably had something to do with it. He had discovered that while I was staying with my uncle I used to visit clandestinely at night a pastor in the neighbouring village. I had got to know Captain Isaac of the Salvation Army and we used to meet for prayer. Hussain Ali had come to know of these meetings. Obviously this could not be allowed to go on.

Lahore was chosen because of the river Ravi which has the reputation of sweeping people into its currents and putting an early end to their earthly journey. Corpses which were dumped into it were carried far away downstream. The Ravi has been fulfilling this function for ages but a climax was reached in 1947 when hundreds of corpses of Muslims were brought along by it from the Gurdaspur and Pathankot districts in India. While I was in Lahore my family did not say or do anything publicly which would have made my conversion known to all our other relatives. I was able during this time to get in touch with Wootton Sahib by mail and one day a missionary brother named Douglas managed to find me. He had been asking for me by my Christian name 'Ghulam Masih' (servant of Christ) and of course, no one knew me by this name. When I saw him standing in the Bazaar, I went up to him and said, 'I am Ghulam Masih'. He asked how I was and left. News of this meeting soon reached my brother. He and his friends decided that the time had come for more drastic action. They decided that on that very night they would bring this shameful business to an end, once and for all. In this the Ravi was to play its traditional role. I must be consigned to its current in a sack. December 6th was a very cold night. In Lahore, winter nights can be very cold. After the evening meal I was stripped of all my clothing and left only in an undervest and a dhoti (loin cloth). I was then locked up in a cold and empty room. The reason for this was that I should become so numbed with cold as to be unable to offer any resistance.

When they locked me in the room I knew what was going to happen and all I wanted to do was to pray. From the day I became a Christian I developed the habit of memorising the Scriptures. I began to recite the passages of Scripture I knew by heart. Passages such as the 'The Lord is my Shepherd' gave me great comfort. Sometimes I cried, sometimes I recited, but most of the time I talked to the Lord. I knew the Lord was present with me and I knew I would simply have to embrace Him after I was dead. I was torn between joy at being in the Lord's presence and anguish knowing the agonising death I would have to go through. Sometimes I even laughed because I had known the power of the Lord and the idea that my family could put an end to my new life in this way was ludicrous. Never for a moment did I doubt the Lord's goodness. Throughout my life my convictions have guided me. Before I was baptised and simply an enquirer in Gojra I read a lot of Christian literature and had discussions with a Pakistani pastor and my English missionary friend. I also read about Islam at this time and never did I think that I was mistaken in the path I had chosen. I knew that Christianity was true and was for me. I had perfect assurance that after my death I would be with the Lord. Nothing could shake this conviction. I am not the sort of person who could be easily shaken of my convictions. I was thus resolute in my conviction that I had chosen the right path even if now it seemed as if it would come to an inglorious end in this world.

While repeating and finding comfort in the Scriptures I had learnt one section in Paul's letter to the Philippians which now struck me forcibly. It was: 'For I am hard pressed between the two, having a desire to depart and be with Christ, which is far better. Nevertheless to remain in the flesh is more needful for you' (Phil. 1:23, 24). Although I found death attractive because of the glorious life I knew would begin after it, I was now drawn into another direction—to live for the sake of my brothers. I began to think that I ought to want to live for those who were still in darkness. I now wanted to be able to take the light of the Gospel to those of my fellow countrymen who needed the Gospel—the good news of what God had done for mankind in and through the death and resurrection of Jesus Christ. This new conviction was strengthened as I recalled the words of Sadhu Sundar Singh (a converted Sikh): 'It is easy to die for Christ but hard to live because dying takes one or two hours but to live is to die daily.' Slowly but surely, this idea took hold of me and filled me with a strange sensation of exultation. What a wonderful vision appeared before my eyes. Not to die just this once for my Lord but to die daily. How my spirit rejoiced within me as this vision permeated my whole being. The only gain from my death now was to my family. They would no longer be embarrassed by me and my faith in the Lord Jesus Christ. They would even try to blot me out of their memory since remembering me would only bring bitterness.

Now I was torn between wanting to die once only for Christ and to die daily for Him in a life of total commitment and sacrifice. I realised that the sacrifice He made for me in dying upon the cross was so precious and deep that even if I were to die a thousand times a day that would not compare with one drop of his precious blood shed for me. This was a difficult problem to resolve however. I was convinced now that I had to pray earnestly for deliverance. Not because of fear of physical death or anything else but simply that I might live and die daily in witnessing to Him who had loved me and given Himself for me. So my prayer went up:

> My Master and Saviour, my spirit is at peace because I know that after this life I will come to you.
> Then there will be no barrier between you and me.
> But the people, especially those who are involved in this scheming and murderous game, will form the impression that they are putting an end to my life.
> Death is the gateway to life for me; part of me longs to enter it; but my death will mean an end to my witness to your name in this circle. And so, if it is pleasing to you, get me out of here tonight and give me the privilege of proclaiming your many great deeds among men. I should then be able to tell them how you refresh men's spirits even today and in this life give sinful men the assurance of

eternal life. I desire, O Lord, my Master, that just as this tongue of mine issued orders for people to be killed, so from this night I may declare words that give life.

My eyes have seen your power. Now if it please you, take me out of here and tomorrow morning will be a new morning in my life. Escape from this death cell will prove to me that you want to keep me alive as your witness.

O Lord, tonight let me be inwardly cleansed of selfishness and concern for my own life. If you keep me alive, I promise to bind myself to a life of service to you with the sole purpose of bringing glory to your name.

Lord, you do not need my help and service but it will be my delight and privilege to serve you. Just as I was zealous to wipe out people you have created so may I be zealous to bring them to you.

If this be your gracious will then deliver me this very night from this place. Amen.

I found that instead of being frozen, I had beads of perspiration on my forehead!

Someone opened the lock from the outside. I waited patiently, listening for footsteps, expecting someone to enter. When no one came I cautiously looked outside, and saw that the street was completely deserted. It was then that I heard the Lord whispering in my ear, 'Run, I have opened the door for you!' I began to run but I did not know in which direction to run. I had only two friends in Lahore and they were Muslims. I did not know any

Christians in Lahore. I continued to run along the railway line which goes from Lahore in the directio of Raiwind. Just beyond Cantonment station, I tripped and fell into a ditch. I was by now extremely tired and stayed there for the rest of the night. I fell asleep. I was woken up at last at about eleven in the morning by the warm rays of the sun beating down upon me. I got up and began to walk towards Model Town (a wealthy district of Lahore). Looking at the fine buildings I suddenly became acutely conscious of my inadequate dress which contrasted so sharply with my surroundings. Behind Model Town, I saw another village and turned aside to walk towards it.

When I entered the village, there were some children playing in the square. I asked one of them, 'Son, are there any Christians here?' 'Yes,' he replied. 'My father is the minister here; what can we do for you?' 'Take me to your father, please,' I implored. The child took me to his home where I met his father, Captain Samuel of the Salvation Army. I was so relieved. Captain Samuel was very gracious to me when I told him what had happened to me. He assured me that I was quite safe now and that if there were any trouble he would defend me with his own life. We had a short time of prayer together then he showed me to a bed. He then sent for the village doctor who examined me and gave me an injection and some medicines. I stayed with the Captain Sahib for four days and asked for permission to go to Gojra. This kind man also gave me a shirt, a pair of shoes, a shawl and five rupees.

On 15th December I reached Gojra. All my friends were delighted to see me, especially Wootton Sahib, Rev. B. M. Augustine, Boota Masih and Master

Charan Dass. The story of my miraculous escape was the cause for much rejoicing. On Christmas Day, I worshipped along with my friend Bawa Masih in his village with villagers from other outlying areas. Bawa Masih's father and younger sister Grace were very close to me. The most important thing for me was that I now was part of the Christian community. I regarded these poor and deprived people as my near and dear ones. Our love for each other was mutual. Christian fellowship in which there is harmony and mutual trust is a wonderful source of encouragement and help in the growth towards Christian maturity. I was safe among friends who accepted me. There was so much for which I was grateful to God.

9: Evangelising for Christ

In the security and peace of Christian fellowship I
began to contemplate seriously the form my ministry
should take. Until I was converted, my search had
been for personal fulfilment but now my thoughts
turned outwards. I recalled the words of the poet
Ghalib:

> *'No victory will come to love's labour of prayer*
> *Till from selfish passions the soul is washed*
> *clean'.*

My many well-wishers at Gojra had various sugges-
tions. One was that I should go into business while
others thought that I ought to enter the ministry. But
I knew what I wanted to do. I had not forgotten the
resolution I made on the night of my deliverance
from certain death. While praising the Lord for all
He had done for me, I made this further request:

> 'Lord, give me the grace to proclaim your
> wondrous deeds in the world.
> Give me such devotion to you that I may keep
> myself pure even in this sinful world.
> The world may look for me, but give me such

love that I may drown in its depth so that the world cannot find me.

Lighten my path for me as I tread these rocky ways so that I may not stumble and cause shame to come upon your glorious name.'

I became convinced that my work for the Lord should be evangelistic and I decided to begin where I was. With some of the young men from the Hostel I went into the villages around Gojra and began preaching the Gospel. Sometimes Mr. Wootton came along with us but I was not very enthusiastic about him joining us in case it inhibited people from treating me just as they wanted to. In addition I wanted to gauge my own acceptability and effectiveness among the people. The area of my service expanded rapidly and it was not long before I was witnessing in villages all over the Punjab. At first I went on foot. Later a friend bought me a bicycle. People used to call me a Sadhu or Holy Man. I made it my practice always to stay with the poor wherever I went. It was my way of identifying with my fellow Christians. I wanted to share their way of life in every way. If they went without food so did I. My wealthy and comfortable background never was a hindrance to me.

Whenever I went into a new area my policy was always to introduce myself to the pastor of that area so that I did nothing in his parish without first seeking his approval. This meant that I also had the opportunity of speaking and preaching to Christians so that their faith might be strengthened. During my itinerant ministry I arrived one night at an Anglican mission station near Lahore. I was to stay with

112

Canon Stanley Huck and take part in some meetings he was arranging. While I was sitting in his office waiting for him, the Lord spoke clearly to me. He said, 'You should go and give your testimony to your brothers in Lahore. That is the place to start.' It was nine o'clock in the evening. As my only ambition was to be obedient to my Master I had no hesitation in doing what he commanded. I felt compelled to go that very night. I left my bicycle there and took a train to Lahore. When I knocked on his door my brother opened the door. You can imagine the look on his face. Amazed, and yet with a slight glimmer of hope in his eyes, he asked, 'Have you come back?' I suppose he wanted to know not only if I had come back to the family but if I had come back to the faith. 'Yes,' I said. 'I have come back but not to live with you again. I simply want to tell you that the Lord Jesus Christ is the Saviour. He has saved me and I know He can save you also.' His expression immediately changed. Trying hard to control his anger, he replied in the most emphatic way, 'Thank you very much. But we don't want you and we don't need your Lord Jesus. We don't want His salvation either. Goodbye.' With that he shut the door in my face. I was sad but not surprised. I was also relieved that I had fulfilled my duty even though it seemed fruitless.

The Lord's words to me on that night sank deep into me and I became convinced that I should witness among my Muslim friends in my ancestral village of Zaffarawal. When I was a child I remember going to the home of an American missionary and his wife who had a mission station in our village. With other boys I often visited their home and joined in the chorus singing which his wife led. After my conversion I had avoided going to this area but now I wrote to the missionary telling him that I wanted to visit him because it had been shown me by the Lord that my ministry should begin in my village. He was very keen to see me. Consequently, in March 1950 I went to Zaffarawal. When I arrived I learnt to my great sorrow that separation from me had caused such sorrow to my mother that she died a few days before my arrival. I deeply regret that I never saw her before she died. She had no knowledge of the plan to murder me. To her I was still a disturbed person whom she desperately wished she could help. I did not allow this tragedy, however, to deter me from the intention I had to serve the Lord who had brought me to my village again.

After the death of my mother the hatred of my brothers for me grew very deep indeed. They laid various murderous plots for me. While I was staying with the missionary they came several times to invite me to their home. At first I refused; then I asked my friend for his advice. He suggested that I should go but not alone. I should take two friends with me. I followed his advice, and made a visit to my brothers. While we were sitting and talking I noticed a sword on the table next to me. It had been sharpened and prepared for use. I suspected that the object was myself. As I picked it up I thought to myself: 'To kill someone with such a sword you have to kill yourself first; your inner being dies before you raise your hand. It is a sign of weakness.' I put it back into its sheath.

The discussion went on for a long time. My brothers had invited a Maulvi to talk with me. It was useless, however. He had nothing very relevant to say. Finally, we were offered a cup of tea. I took my first sip; it was horribly bitter and I realised immediately that it was poisoned. I was not afraid. I remembered Jesus' words to the disciples after His resurrection that those who believed and were baptised will see many signs. One of these was '. . . if they drink anything deadly, it will by no means hurt them.' (Mark 16:18). I believed that this was my opportunity to experience one of these signs. I drank the remaining tea and prayed, 'Lord, hold me up.' Soon I became restless and felt very dizzy. I told my friends that it was time to go. My brothers did not know how I was feeling. Outside of the town not far from the mission station I told my friends to go ahead and leave me alone. It was ten o'clock at night. I began to pray;

> 'Lord, if I die tonight people will say that
> Christianity is false. It is not me but your
> name which will be dishonoured.'

As soon as I finished praying I was sick twice and all the poison left my system. I then slept peacefully. In the morning I went to the mission station. My brothers were anxious to know what had happened to me and so when I saw someone from the village walking about nearby I knew that he had been sent by them. I recognised him as one of their servants and told him to go and tell my family that I was alive.

It was not only my faith which was an embarrassment to my family. My brothers were also afraid that I would now claim my share in the inheritance. They made another attempt on my life. While I was on a visit to Narowal a Muslim friend of mine arrived at the home of the Rev. Isaac Dass to tell me that some Kashmiri youths were waiting for me at the toll-bridge. I resolved that I would steer clear of all those things which could adversely affect my resolve to serve the Lord and so I declared formally in writing that I renounced all claim to the estate of my father, Chaudhry Lal Khan, in favour of my brothers. Thus I severed all ties with my family. They had nothing to fear from me now. Perhaps they would leave me alone to live my life of witnessing. But it gradually became obvious to me that my life was not safe in the Punjab. I had begun my ministry there as I had been told to do but there was no reason why I should remain there. It was during this time of reflection that I met a very kind and loving friend, the Rev. Chandu Ray, later Bishop Chandu Ray. We had a long conversation about my ministry. He advised me to go to Sukkur in Sind. I accepted his advice, remembering the words of Bulhe Shah, the Punjabi poet:

'Come on Bulhe, let us go to a place
Where no one knows our caste, or pays us any
    special attention.'

The missionary at Sukkur at this time was the venerable Carson-Sahib. For a few months I worked for the Bible Society. This work involved some administration and writing-up of reports. I became very troubled however; my heart was not in this kind of work. Moreover, I began to feel that I was getting too commercially orientated. I felt uneasy; I was straying from my original vision. I decided to relinquish my post.

I saw myself as an evangelist and therefore I had to equip myself for this task. I started learning Sindhi with the help of Padre Carson. Very quickly, and with not too much effort, I mastered Sindhi and began to speak, write and read it fluently. The language barrier was now removed and I was able to join Mr. Carson in his evangelistic work. There was one setback to my work in Sukkur. The summer season began and the heat proved too much for me. Although I had made up my mind that Sind was to be the sphere of my ministry, I had to leave it for a while.

I returned to the Punjab. While I was there, I met an American pastor by the name of Leroy Selby at Lyallpur (now Faisalabad). He invited me to join him in working among the young people. The Lyallpur Convention had only just begun. For the first two years of its existence this convention was essentially a youth convention. I had nowhere to stay and because I did not like living with missionaries, I made arrangements to stay with a Christian, Chaudhry Jalal Masih. He was a gracious man and was almost like a father to me. I was accepted as one of the family and his son and daughter treated me as a brother. This relationship opened the doors of the community for me and I became even more engrossed in my service for the Lord. From this base in Lyallpur I went all over the country on my bicycle. I covered about 12,000 miles travelling several times between Kemari (in Karachi) to the south and Landi Kotal (near Peshawar on the Afghan border) to the north.

I remember once I was taken to a small town by an American friend. He was a Reformed Presbyterian missionary. I was asked to preach at a service he was conducting. During the service when the time came for the collection I found myself having a mental struggle. When I felt in my pockets all I had was eight annas or half a rupee. What could I do? I needed that money and yet I could not let the collection plate pass by without putting something in it. When it came to me I had no choice. I simply put my hand in my pocket, took the eight annas out and dropped them on the plate. The battle was over. The service concluded but I kept on wondering what I could do without any money. Little did I know that within a short time I was to experience God's wonderful provision again.

I returned to the home of one of my Pakistani friends. His wife met me with the message, 'Brother, somebody wanted to see you.' I was most surprised; I had expected no one. Then she told me that two nurses from the hospital came to see me because they knew I was leaving the next day. They were sorry they had missed the service and left an envelope for me. When I took it to my room and opened it there was a bundle of rupees in it with a note saying, 'The Lord has shown us that you need money for your travel. Please take this and be thankful.' I was speechless. God was truly a good God.

Towards the end of the summer I returned to Sind. I began work as an evangelist among the Hindu tribes of Mewasi and Bhil. After partition many Hindus remained in the province of Sind. Once again however, I was faced with a language problem. They spoke Gujarati. I didn't. I was determined to remove any barrier to my work if I could. Since I found learning languages easy I was able to master it within a few months. In taking the message of the Gospel to these people I found that my previous experience of Hinduism was invaluable. I knew some Hindu religious practices. Some of these I had had to observe myself in the first Hindu secondary school I attended. The fact that I knew by heart some of the Hindu mantras was also a great help. Even the skill I had acquired as a child of playing the harmonium added a pleasing dimension to my ministry because the Hindus love the harmonium. I bought one for fifty rupees and took it round on my bicycle as I went from village to village presenting the Gospel of Jesus Christ.

With the help of three associates I worked continuously for two years among these Hindu tribes. For all of this time I lived under a banyan tree and sometimes in a little hut. One night I took a projector on my bicycle to show a film strip of the life of Jesus. The people were not very enthusiastic and I did not feel very welcome in their presence. Afterwards two gentlemen led me to a straw hut in which I could spend the rest of the night. I usually had with me on these occasions a single linen sheet to spread on the ground. That was my bed. The next morning one member of the tribes—Jivah—a bold and intelligent man, was passing by this hut. He was amazed that I had been put there to sleep for during the day the men who worked in the fields used it as a lavatory. I said that I did not mind since it was the only place offered to me. He was shocked and thought that they were a despicable people not to have offered me suitable accommodation. I was able to lead this man to Christ and later he also became an evangelist. He was a deeply humble man and full of the Spirit.

Unfortunately, he died within eighteen months. But he left a mark on those he tried to evangelise.

Seemingly my humility had touched him but I knew that my humiliation was nothing compared to the humiliation of my Saviour upon the cross. God's love and goodness were revealed in his weakness. If I wanted to be used so that his love and goodness shine in my life then I too must be counted as least among men and treated as such. I was merely imitating my Lord. It was my lifestyle above all which appealed to these poor people and attracted them to me, and made it possible to tell them the good news of God's salvation. As a sign of purity and simplicity I dressed like a Hindu Sadhu. I earned no salary and lived only on what was given to me.

I soon realised that one of the most fruitful ways to do my evangelising was to teach the people to read. One does not often realise how dependent the Christian faith is upon a book. It is true that its primary emphasis is upon a personal relationship with God, based on forgiveness and reconciliation. But the revelation of God's love and salvation is written in a book. Illiterate people can only grasp the basis of this faith from other people and from personal experience. To grow and become mature Christians, who can then tell others of their faith, they need to be able to read. To this end I began adult literacy classes. Gradually, the door to people's minds and homes began to be opened to me. They were beginning to find me useful. One day I was called to a village to pray for a very sick child. The child recovered. On another occasion I was asked to go and pray for an old lady. She also was healed. These poor, illiterate people could see that our Lord does hear and answer prayers. They were anxious to learn to pray. I was never tempted to use prayer merely to work miracles. This would have reduced my faith to magic, and dishonoured our Lord. I believe that when doors are closed, God opens them. If miracles would do it then miracles do happen. It would have been so easy for me to use God in this way but I knew that this would be one way of lifting up myself and not the Lord. It would have been contrary to my whole policy which was always to count myself as nothing, so that in all things He alone may be exalted.

Women always seem to respond more quickly to the Gospel. They have such a key role in the home that their conversions nearly always mean a transformation of the home. Young girls were also very anxious to learn to read, so that they could read the Bible for themselves. It was not unusual for me to become the object of attraction to some of them. This was never my intention. Sometimes the misunderstanding and even hatred that resulted from trying to help the poor educate their children were the bitter fruit I reaped. Nearly always I used money which was given to me for my personal use for this purpose.

There was a beautiful young girl from one of the tribes who started to read the Gospels. Gradually I noticed signs of special concern for me. Her simplicity sometimes amused me as when, for example, she asked me to wear my sandals instead of my shoes so she could see my heels! I was very moved by her devotion and I was also attracted to her. It was not a relationship which could be encouraged, however. There was too much between us that would have hindered a closer friendship. Furthermore, her father had other plans for her. He wanted her to marry a man who was already married but who had no children. To make matters worse the man was a certified tuberculosis case. This poor girl wept bitterly and pleaded with me to help her: 'Please Maharaj (guru or teacher) help me. I don't want to marry a sick old man. He is a Hindu. I am a Christian and I love the Lord.' I was helpless. I longed to help her and take her out of her miserable existence. This happened so often and I was unable to do anything. There were not many young Christian men about who could have married her. Her father was a very determined man and it was useless to reason with him. She was beaten into submission.

A few years later when I returned to Sind I borrowed a motor cycle from one of my Christian friends and went to her village. The evening sun was setting as I arrived. As I looked in the distance towards the sinking sun I could see flames rising from a funeral pyre. A group of people were returning to the village from it. Among them I recognised the brother of the young girl. I learnt from him that his sister Devi had died and that this was her funeral pyre I could see. I was so grieved. This was the second time in my life that I had arrived on the funeral day of a person who had been dear to me.

As the sun rises in the east
And sets in the west
So must all our lives be
A rising and a setting.
While in this mortal frame we be.

122

But in that final glorious sunset,
When all mortal beings cease to be
We shall rise to set no more
For in Him who has conquered death
We shall live for evermore.

I do not think that my work among these Hindu
tribes had been a failure despite great disappointments. There were some encouraging signs as the
people began to understand the Gospel. Those who
were truly converted smashed their clay idols, and
stopped lying and cheating. No more did they sell
their daughters or force them to marry men who were
already married.

During this period of my ministry I occasionally
had contacts with people who did not belong to these
tribes. One such occasion is indelibly printed on my
memory. I had decided to visit a man who had shown
some interest in the Christian faith. I went to his
town but failed to find him. Disappointed and tired,
I got into a bus to return to the station. Sitting next to
me on the bus was an old Muslim man and we got
into conversation. He started questioning me about
myself and when I told him I was an evangelist he
was excited and delighted. I was somewhat puzzled.
But it seems that I was God's answer to his prayer.
Muslims usually aim to make one visit at least to
Mecca. He had been seven times and yet he did not
find what he was looking for. He told me that someone had given him a copy of the Gospels in his own
language and he had been reading them. Like the
Ethiopian eunuch in the Acts of the Apostles he
needed someone to explain it to him. Here he was on
this bus praying that God would send someone and I

was sitting by his side. When I learnt this all the weariness fell off and I accepted joyfully the privilege of explaining the Gospel to him. When we arrived at his stop he invited me to his home. He was a landlord and owned 7,000 acres of land. After a long conversation in his huge house he asked me to pray for him. I told him to pray for himself. He seemed very surprised and asked, 'Can I?' 'Yes' I replied, 'if you can talk to me you can talk to God.' Then he said, 'Lord Jesus, thank you for sending me your servant, for leading me in the right path. Please accept me; I take you for my Saviour from today.' I knew that God had accepted him. There is no limit to God's goodness and generosity. All those who call upon the Lord are truly saved.

10: Following a New Path

I do believe that I was keeping my promise to my Saviour to be His witness. For seven years I went about as an evangelist taking the message of the Gospel to those who had never heard it. Of my three associates, two of them have remained faithful and are still in the field. One sadly has fallen away. But the time seemed to have come for me to take another direction. While my work as an evangelist was valued, there were those among my friends and the clergy who felt that I would be a more useful and effective witness if I had theological training and entered the ordained ministry. The Bishop of Lahore was particularly instrumental in the decision I made to go for theological training. Remembering St. Paul's words to Timothy: 'Study to show thyself approved unto God, a workman that needeth not to be ashamed, rightly dividing the word of truth' (2 Timothy 2:15). I welcomed the opportunity to have a good theological training.

Before I went away for my theological training a dear lady came to me. She obviously felt very concerned for me. 'My good man,' she said, 'you will find fighting your emotions a very costly business. Your self-control will be broken. You hold in your

125

hand a rosary but its thread is at breaking point. When it breaks the beautiful beads will be scattered and everyone will laugh at you.' This was her way of saying that I might fall prey to temptation and lose my faith. 'How long are you going to roam about with the flickering shadows of these trees as your only protection? Take someone as your partner in prayer.'

She was right but up to this point in my life I had resisted any thought of marriage. I felt that I should not allow personal happiness to take precedence over my mission in life. Besides, living more or less like a 'rolling stone' there could be no place for a wife in my life.

In 1955 I entered Theological College in Gujranawala as a single man. It was not the easiest of situations for me. My financial resources were very slim indeed. Unlike the other students who received help from their families I was all alone with no resources to draw upon. The scholarship I received from the College amounted to thirty rupees. Yet I continued my practice of tithing. I had been given a conditional entrance to the College. At the end of the first term examinations were to be held which would determine whether I would be allowed to continue with my training. However, I was a hard worker and had no difficulty in passing these examinations. Of course, had anyone taken the trouble to examine my past before I became a Christian they would have discovered that I was quite capable of study. Anyway, the authorities soon recognised my abilities. I had a good memory and this was of immense help to me. Soon I was gaining top marks in all my subjects and various prizes came my way.

Although I was beginning to find my feet and enjoyed theological studies, I never lost my original simplicity and vision of what my life's work must be. My love for my Saviour grew daily. In October 1955 I decided to adopt the name 'Naaman'. Naaman was the name of the Syrian leper in the Old Testament who was healed miraculously. I took this name because I wanted a perpetual reminder of my past. I too had been cleansed and healed—of sin—and I did not want to forget it. It was to be the rock upon which I stood as I witnessed to the Lord.

In my second year at College my friends began to encourage me to get married so that my wife could also have some theological training. My thoughts turned to Daisy. My first encounter with her had been on an unplanned visit to Karachi with a New Zealand missionary. She had asked me to address the nurses. I had chosen for my subject the story of Lazarus. My opening words were: 'The Lord whom you love is sick; the Lord whom you love is dead.' For some inexplicable reason two of the nurses started giggling and whispering. I asked them to leave the room. Naturally, they were displeased to be embarrassed before their colleagues. One of these nurses was Daisy. I also noticed that on my subsequent visits to Karachi that Daisy was always at my meetings. She showed much interest in me and was concerned about my state of poverty. Sometimes she went so far as to buy me a shirt. During a conversation with her one day I said, 'Miss, I wish every young girl could marry and set up a Christian home. We need Christian homes.' She responded with, 'Whom shall I marry?' 'I don't know,' I replied rather meekly. 'How about you?' she boldly asked.

She took me by surprise; I wasn't prepared for such an answer. 'I have no home. I have nothing,' I said. She didn't seem deterred by this. 'I have a home and money,' she insisted. It was getting too involved. 'I don't want just a wife; any ordinary woman can become a wife. I need a person to be a real companion to me,' I replied. Back came her response, 'I will be your companion.' I wasn't going to give up easily in trying to extricate myself from what had become a very delicate situation so I said, 'I think we have gone far enough. Let us leave this affair in God's hands.'

Daisy was a fully qualified nurse with a good job and the prospect of going abroad and gaining more experience. She was a member of the World Health Organisation and had been put in charge of the health visitor training scheme. Would she accept?

I had to go north to a conference arranged by Mr. Kenneth Cragg in the Punjab. While I was there Daisy's brother invited me to their home in Sialkot. I accepted his invitation. When I arrived I was most surprised to find Daisy there. She had taken seven days leave to go up to see her family. The whole family was extremely kind to me and asked me to stay with them for the rest of my time in the Punjab. Before I left I had no doubt about the family's hopes for Daisy and me. I think I had underestimated her and her commitment to Jesus Christ. She too had a burning desire to witness for her Lord and she was not afraid of the austere life style I had chosen for myself. In fact she was impressed and wanted to share it. In December 1955 we got engaged.

The occasion of our engagement was joyful in more ways than one for me. Among the friends gathered together to celebrate with us was the American missionary who had a mission station in Zaffarawal. This man, whose sermons I could not understand as a child, was one of God's instruments in bringing me to Christ but I had no idea of it. During the evening he got up and said, 'Tonight, my heart is overflowing with joy. When I first set my eyes upon this young man eighteen years ago I prayed, "Lord, I want him for you."' God had answered his prayer so wonderfully. I was humbled. The fact that my Saviour had been seeking for me and had begun His work in my life without my having the slightest knowledge of it, had a strange effect upon me. 'Who can trace the hand of destiny?'

Our wedding was due to take place on October 8th, 1956. I was almost destitute but I trusted the Lord to provide for my needs. On October 5th I went up to Sialkot, Daisy's home town. My brother owned a factory in that town so I decided to visit him. While in his office talking he soon became aware of my poor situation. Despite all that had happened in the past, brotherly love and, I dare say, self-interest, led him to make me a generous gift of money. He did not want the family name disgraced. Many of the workers in his factory were Christians. Sialkot has a large Christian population. How tempting it was to take the money. My situation was bleak indeed and I could not see where I would get money from for my wedding. But He who gives us His grace in our weakness, did not fail me. He gave me the courage to refuse and assurance that He would supply my needs. I was able once again to witness to my brother and said to him, 'Jesus Christ will take care of me and supply the money I need.' Then I left.

My room mate was by now getting agitated. The wedding was in two days time. I had no decent clothes nor any money for food. On the evening of October 6th we went to a volleyball game. While we were there a bearer from an American Missions Treasury Office gave me an envelope from a Mr. Steward. I put the envelope in my pocket. Later, in my room, when I opened it there was no letter in it, only money. God had again provided. I shared this with Daisy after we were married and we both felt that this was a happy omen for us; God was blessing our union.

It was now possible for the preparations to begin. With the money the Vice-Principal's wife helped me to get all that was necessary. My 'father' in Lyallpur, Chaudry Jalal Masih, and another friend came to make all the necessary arrangements. Daisy and I were happily married in College on October 8th, 1956.

Financially, life was not easy for us. Daisy came from a wealthy family but did not like to ask for assistance. We tried to live on what I had, which was very little. On one occasion we were severely tested. We had no food for two days. Daisy's faith began to waver. I have no doubt that she asked herself why she had married someone like me. She must have been tempted many a time to return to her parents. Unlike my family, hers would have welcomed her. They were Christians. I had no one to turn to. But I had never seen God's children 'begging bread' (Psalm 37:25) and tried to reassure her, reminding her of God's gracious provision in the past.

On the third day of our 'enforced fast' we were in a service with other students and their wives. At the end of the service the Principal of Daisy's seminary gave me a blue envelope. When we got back to our room and opened it we discovered that a friend from New Zealand had sent us seventy-five rupees. This, she said, was her wedding present to us. She had not been able to send it earlier. All we could do was to get down on our knees and thank our wonderful Creator for His goodness to us. Once again He had kept His promise. His faithfulness caused us to rejoice in Him and praise His name.

Our testing was not yet over, however. It is customary during one's theological training to do some practical evangelism. When I went up to the Principal to get details of my assignment I noticed that he looked rather apologetic. I wondered what was troubling him. He seemed reluctant to tell me about the field I was to work in. All the other assignments had been taken, he said, and only one remained. 'What is it?' I asked wondering why he was hesitating. Then he told me. I was to work among a Hindu tribe—the untouchables. This particular tribe earned its livelihood by going round and picking up dirty rags. These they washed and sold for use in cleaning machinery. They lived in hand-made tents and usually lots of feathers were to be seen around their tents. The reason for this was because they used to pick up dead chickens wherever they found them and cook them for their food. They lived like gypsies. My job was to evangelise them, to take them the Gospel of the love of God. The Principal seemed slightly surprised and relieved when I said I would go.

My desire and commitment was to witness to my Saviour to everyone rich and poor, high and low. To me these distinctions are of no relevance. All men need to be saved. These people needed the Gospel and I would take it to them. Would Daisy come with me? Men were allowed to take their wives along with them. To my great joy she did, without any persuasion from me. It was the beginning of a shared ministry which has lasted until the present day.

This Gaghra tribe only spoke Marwasi, a dialect of Punjabi. I established adult literacy classes and began to teach them Urdu. My mother tongue was Dogri but I also speak Urdu, Punjabi, Persian, Arabic, Gujarati, Pashto, Hindi and English. I tried to identify with these people but at first they were hesitant in their response to me. Gradually they drew closer and began to offer me hospitality. Just a glass of water to start with but it was such a great step forward that I even consented to drink from one of their glasses. The ultimate act of acceptance on both sides was when they offered me curried dead chickens and I ate them. A door was flung open by that simple act.

Daisy and I graduated from seminary in March 1958 having passed our examinations with distinction. Our crowning joy, however, was to see on our graduation day the Pakistani Pastor baptising eight families, about sixty people, from this poor tribe. Their distinctive mark from now on was not the eating of dead chickens, a practice which they gave up and thus earned the respect of everyone, but the sign of the cross made on their foreheads by the Pastor. How thrilled we were. What better way to finish college than to see right from the start of our ministry the Spirit of God working through us to reach even the lowest of the low with His love and mercy.

We were happy after our seminary days to return to Sind and work among the Hindu tribes I already knew. But Bishop Chandu Ray felt that for Daisy's sake, as she was new to this kind of work, we should have a more gentle start. After my ordination in Lahore Cathedral by Bishop Woolmer, we were sent to Hyderabad. I was now a deacon and worked under the supervision of the Rev. Jewan Rawar. He was a good priest and was a great help to me in those early days. For nearly two years I worked under him doing evangelistic and pastoral work. I had the opportunity of evangelising tribal people who spoke Gujarati. This time there was no language difficulty as I already knew Gujarati. But Daisy had to learn. She began with conversational Gujarati so that she could converse with women in their own language and work alongside me. She saw this as a great calling because, like me, she felt strongly the need for women to be converted. Very often the whole family atmosphere the Christian woman is able to create is permeated with Christian values and standards. Daisy therefore made the women's needs, physical and spiritual, her main concern. Her qualifications and experience as a nurse proved invaluable to her. As a result of her contribution we were able to reach whole households rather than just individuals.

Apart from work among the tribe, I now had pastoral duties. These were new to me since this was the first time in my life of witness that I was working in a settled community and not moving from place to place as an evangelist. My initiation into this type of work was marred by one very unpleasant incident. I was asked by the Christian congregation to baptise two children. When I enquired about the father of the children I learnt that he was a Muslim. The mother, a Christian young woman, had married a Muslim and now she wanted me to baptise the children of the marriage. I felt I could not do this until she had made a public confession of her mistake in marrying a Muslim. This may seem a harsh step to have asked her to take, but in a country where Christians are in a minority, that minority needs to uphold certain standards for its own survival as well as to maintain its distinctiveness. The mother refused to do as I asked and her whole family turned against me. They made all sorts of false accusations against me. They even accused me of trying to win her affection. This affair created much bitterness and hatred and division in the congregation. The result was that my ordination to the priesthood (normally one year after ordination to the diaconate) was postponed for six months. I had been used to persecution of one kind or another most of my life but when the wound is made by Christians it nearly always seems more painful. I was disappointed over the postponement of my ordination as priest (presbyter). However, it gave me time for reflection and the seriousness of ordination to the priesthood impressed itself more and more upon me. Now it became not just another step in the chain of events leading to a fully ordained ministry but something very special.

After my ordination, we left Hyderabad in February 1960 and went to Mirpur Khas. This was a desert area. Most of the people were tenant farmers and were caught in the grip of unpaid debts. They borrowed loans to cultivate their fields and then the landlords took their harvest as payment of their debts. These poor tenants had to resort to loans for food and so the vicious circle tightened its grip upon them. Generation after generation inherited debts from which they could not release themselves.

On many occasions I was forced to intervene on behalf of some peasant. As I became more and more respected in the community, even the Hindus and Muslims sought my help. My belief is that God saves the whole man and not just part of him. All man's needs therefore, whether they are spiritual, social or economic are important. I saw it as part of my ministry to seek justice for them and alleviate their suffering whenever I could.

The lack of education was appalling and I did what had by now come to be a necessary part of my ministry. I held adult literacy classes and I encouraged the parents to send their children to school. They were reluctant to do this. Some feared that the children would eventually leave them if they became educated. In a country where a lonely old age in desperate poverty is feared, children are a kind of insurance, a means of guaranteed security. In addition, children were needed to work in the fields. I felt I could get nowhere with such people unless I helped them to become literate. With this aim in mind I started a hostel for boys in my home. They shared our food and we provided them with clothing. To start with there were only six of them. These boys later became civil servants or engineers. The Diocese eventually expanded this work and established a hostel for one hundred and fifty boys.

We now had a family of our own. Our son Samuel was born on September 19th, 1960. His birth was a direct answer to our prayer. I remember that on December 19th, 1959, the day before my ordination,

Daisy and I prayed for a son. Exactly nine months later Samuel arrived. On the day we brought him home from hospital, instead of going straight into our house we took him to the church and placed him on the holy table and dedicated him to the Lord. For me it was a great beginning. My adopted name 'Naaman' with all its meaning of cleansing and healing, was now going to be borne by my son. It was a living witness to what the Lord had done for me. On April 17th, 1962 our household was again blessed by the arrival of a beautiful daughter, Khulda.

That same year however I saw also the beginning of physical pain and suffering in my life. I began to have kidney problems. It was my usual habit to drink untreated water from the canal and as a result I developed kidney stones.

My physical pain did not affect me as deeply however as the pain I suffered at the hands of a young man, John Mohammed Ali. He was sent to me by a missionary friend so that I could provide a home for him and teach him the Christian faith. As a convert Mohammed Ali's life in Karachi had been intolerable. Remembering my own past when I was, like him, without home or friends, I welcomed him into my home and treated him as one of the family. I was aware that he was a very immature Christian and was not to be trusted but I believed it was right for me to give him the opportunity to amend his ways. My own faith was in Jesus Christ our Lord who did not reject Judas although He knew that Judas would betray Him.

One day while I was on my tour in the villages along with my junior priest, this young man left my home, taking all my good books, Daisy's jewellery,

136

our money and all my priestly garments. The theft was reported to the police because a Webley Scot pistol belonging to one of my Muslim friends was also taken. Of all the things stolen my books were the most precious to me. They were books which had been given to me as gifts to help me in my ministry. I had three sets of commentaries on the Quran in Urdu and in English, and two sets of *Traditions* or *Hadeeds*.

I later learnt that this young man had been sent by a group of Muslim religious leaders with the express purpose of destroying my library. Their hope was to make me an ineffective worker for the Lord. He had obviously deceived my missionary friend. I was most upset by his deception and the length to which people would go to obliterate my Christian faith. I accepted it all as part of the sacrifice I was called upon to make. My promise to die daily for my Lord was being kept.

My kidney problem was getting worse and I was advised to leave this area. The authorities decided to send me to Quetta near the Afghan border. Quetta is over 5,000 feet above sea level. At first I worked with Padre Inayat Rumal Shah who was vicar of Quetta. It was good to meet him again. He was the one to whom I had been sent by the old sweeper on the railway platform. He tried to teach me Anglican discipline. I recall one very embarrassing service when I arrived two minutes late—I had to arrive half an hour before the first bell rang. He promptly told me to take my cassock off and sit in the congregation. I did so, reluctantly. I was never late again! But I was to be embarrassed once again; this time by his family. The Padre had gone to India to attend a conference. He left me in charge. His son who was a student in Bishop's College, Calcutta, was home on vacation. He wanted me to accompany him to the cinema. It was not my habit to go to the movies but *Lawrence of Arabia* was on and I succumbed to the temptation. His sisters were very upset that we did not allow them to accompany us. In the middle of the film, I heard my name being shouted above all the noise of the movie. 'Padre Naaman, Padre Naaman, there is a funeral.' Over and over it came and everyone started to look for us. This was his sisters' idea of a joke. It was a genuine call, however, and I crawled out sheepishly to take it. Funerals in most hot countries have to be within twenty-four hours of death.

Wherever I went I seemed to be challenged to learn a new language. The Pathans speak Pashto and in order to be able to communicate with them I had to learn it. In some ways I enjoyed the challenge. While I was in Quetta my kidney deteriorated and it was found necessary to have it removed. That was, however, to be the end of my kidney problems.

I was appointed Chaplain to the hospital in Quetta where nomadic Afghan tribesmen were catered for. The work was varied and interesting. I was a pastor to the hospital staff, an evangelist to the Muslim patients and a youth leader to the young male student nurses. My family was also growing; a second son, Obed Nayer, was born in 1963, so my responsibilities as a father increased. Not surprisingly perhaps, the strain of all my different roles began to take their toll. In 1965 I suffered my first heart attack. It was a serious one. After a few months of convalescence the doctors recommended that I should return to the plains. We returned to Mirpur Khas.

138

This was a time of great mental and spiritual struggle for me. It seemed that my life's work was to be abruptly ended. I had been advised to spend much of my time in bed and not do any travelling if I wanted to make a good recovery. It seemed that my life of witnessing was over. For most of my life I had had good health. It was not that I feared death or could not bear suffering. I welcomed suffering and I wanted to die daily for my Lord. This was what I had promised to do. Had I failed to realise my ambition? Had I failed my Lord? Such questions kept rising up in my mind. In this state of mind I prayed earnestly for some guidance. Prayer has always been a very important part of my life. I find the early morning a wonderful time for prayer and meditation. It is during these times that I draw close to my Lord. I do not believe, as many immature Christians seem to do, that one must petition God for one need after another. As a father I know what my children's needs are and I try to meet them. God would not do less for us. So I did not pray for healing and relief from pain and suffering but only for understanding as to how I could serve my Lord in my stricken state. I wanted to know how I could continue my life of witness. As always, He answered my prayer. 'Naaman,' He said, 'so far you have always taken me as the Lord of your soul. Now I have touched your body to show you that I am Lord of your body as well. You don't have to go out to witness to me. Sit and think. Write out the experiences you have had.' I bowed before Him. Truly God's hands were upon me. He was faithful to His promises, and was going to manifest His power in my weakness. People began coming to me and hundreds accepted the Lord. One particular conversion meant a great deal to me. A man from the Bhil tribe, Dadu, was converted during this time in my ministry. I mention him because since I had first met him way back in 1953 I had prayed for his conversion. His father and brothers had accepted the Lord and were baptised. Somehow he himself had never 'made it'. But in 1967 he finally accepted the Lord as his Saviour and became my helper. Now he is a priest.

I felt immensely privileged to be able to spend time writing. I began the story of my life and also contributed to various magazines. My earlier attempts at poetry now became more sustained and systematic. For the first time in my life I had opportunity to give rein to my creative instincts and began writing radio plays and novels.

I had found a new turn to my vocation but my domestic situation was rather bleak. I was not paid much since there was another priest at Mirpur Khas. With three young children to bring up, Daisy found it very difficult to cope financially. She decided to return to nursing. She saw her work in the hospital as her witness to the Lord so that it was not merely for financial gain that she went. Fortunately she was able to work in the local Roman Catholic hospital as a nursing tutor. She worked from 9 a.m. to noon. During this time a near tragedy took place. Of course she did not tell me at the time because of my health.

It was her habit in the mornings to leave a flask of tea and some biscuits by my bedside for the children and especially the youngest who was only two. One day the child followed her without her knowing. While she was in the middle of a class someone came to tell her that her son had nearly drowned and had been brought to the hospital. While he was following her he had fallen into a drain. Open drains are very common in Pakistan. Alarmed, she went to the children's ward. She could not see him anywhere. Then one of the nurses told her that he was in the doctor's room on oxygen. When she saw him he was almost blue. Distressed and deeply shocked, the full reality of her desperate situation dawned on her. Our God did not fail us, however. He took care of us. The hospital authorities were very kind and offered Daisy a room in the hospital where our two-year old could play while she was teaching.

While Daisy's employment alleviated our poverty we were soon to suffer another financial blow. I once again took two young men from Hindu families into my home. They stayed for a while, shared our hospitality and then left. Within a week of leaving, they returned and broke into our house. They stole all the money I had in a steel cabinet. This money belonged to one of the villagers who had entrusted it to me for safekeeping. To return the villager's money I had to borrow two thousand rupees from my Diocese. This money had to be repaid from my small salary and a sum was deducted from it each month. Thus we were in terrible financial straits.

My evangelistic work was difficult but the response of the people was most encouraging and kept me going even in the most difficult moments. And there were no shortage of these. During the whole period from November 1965 to July 1973 I spent my own money on travelling from village to village, paying hospital bills for those who were ill and couldn't afford to pay them because I believed that this was right. I expected to be reimbursed by the Diocese. To my amazement the person in charge of the distribution of charity, a

141

notable figure in the Church in Pakistan, refused to allow me to be repaid. When I received the bill for 8,000 rupees I was deeply shocked and hurt. This was a great blow to my already impoverished family. It was a most painful experience to me—almost a 'financial death'. To receive such treatment from the hands of someone I regarded as a friend was so distressing. During these times of hardship and poverty I looked only to Him who Himself was rewarded with a shameful death on the cross despite His great love and sacrifice for man. And the Lord provided.

While fruitful in many ways, my ministry in Mirpur Khas could not continue. In addition to my difficult financial situation, it was felt that I was putting my remaining kidney at risk by staying where I was since the water in the area was unsuitable for me. My Bishop decided to send me to Sukkur in Sind where I had first begun my ministry.

11: All for Jesus

I arrived in Sukkur in July 1973 to be the Vicar of St. Saviour's Church. This was my first real pastoral job. Except for the two periods in Hyderabad and Mirpur Khas where I did some pastoral work my work had been mainly that of an evangelist. I found it a real challenge. No longer was I able to travel around, preaching the Gospel, and leaving believers to the care of others. It was now my responsibility to care for converts and build up the church.

I must confess that for the first two years it was an uphill struggle. Relationships with my congregation seemed so superficial. People were unwilling to draw me into their confidence and I could not enter into their lives, and share their difficulties. Pakistanis are naturally reticent with strangers over their personal affairs. They do not easily let strangers know of their personal difficulties. Gradually, however, as we got to know eath other better, the barriers began to come down and the beginnings of real Christian fellowship started to appear. In some cases I had to take the initiative and enter into situations where I felt I had to take a stand. For example, I learnt from my family that a Christian boy and girl wanted to get married but their parents objected. Arranged marriages are

143

still the norm in Pakistan and parents decide who their children should marry. Since the family unit is so important, families do not join together without much preliminary investigations into each other's background. The parents of the bride and groom have to meet each other and decide for themselves whether the other's family is suitable for a daughter or son to enter. Increasingly, however, as young men and women become educated and liberated, they demand choice for themselves. This couple were typical of the new generation of young people. Instead of coming to me, this young couple sought a Maulvi or Muslim priest to perform the marriage ceremony. To do this the priest would first have insisted on the couple renouncing their Christianity and becoming Muslims. As soon as I learnt about this I went to the boy's home, called all the relatives together and married the couple on that very day. I was of course very disappointed that the couple had not turned to me in the first place. They later said that they were afraid to come to me. I suppose they thought I would be on their parents' side, and would also have objected to the marriage. But Christian homes are so precious and important that unless the parents had very good reasons for objecting I do not see how I would not have helped them. This couple now have two children and a lovely Christian home.

On another occasion I was confronted with an even more difficult situation. A Muslim boy and a Christian girl were living together. I felt that this was wrong and challenged the man to leave the Christian girl or become a Christian. He was not antagonistic to Christianity and attended services occasionally but he refused to become a committed Christian. The girl was willing to terminate the relationship unless he made a definite decision. At the end of one week he decided to become a Christian and was baptised. Later they were married in church.

Marriage difficulties form one area where it is possible to get close to people. Sometimes they are amusing. On one occasion I went to conduct the marriage ceremony of a couple who were already living together in the father-in-law's house. When I arrived, the groom's father was working in the field. He had forgotten all about it! After the ceremony he stayed out in the field for the whole night to avoid paying me the small fee!

It is so important in an Islamic country to have definite Christian standards of morality. Conversion from Islam to Christianity could at one time be punished by death. With the spread of Western liberal ideas in Islamic countries, a change was almost inevitable. International opinion was important and could not be ignored. So the death penalty was eventually abolished and Islam was forced to reconstruct its religious thought and system. Before this, when the authorities took no action, a convert could be murdered by his own relatives as would have happened in my case. But I can sense a change in the air now. Pakistan is gradually being Islamicised. Eventually only the Quranic and Islamic law will be observed in this country. From my observation of the political and social scene, it seems obvious that the death penalty for conversion will be reintroduced. While the political authorities are distracted by provincial and external problems they have allowed conversions to take place with impunity. But the time will come when they will direct their attention to the problem of converts and Christians will once again be threatened. I cannot see 'Murtadds' (i.e. people who denounce Islam) being tolerated for long. If I should be among them I will accept my destiny willingly. God is in control and if this is the way He will be glorified in my life then it will be my privilege to honour Him.

It is very costly nevertheless for a Muslim to become a Christian. Even when one's life is not at stake, as now, the ostracism and isolation can be very painful. The cultural readjustment which has to take place often goes on for the rest of the convert's life because he has to move in circles where oriental habits and customs have often to be suppressed in favour of a western sub-culture. Even his vocabulary has to change. A Christian in Pakistan for example, finds that the ordinary Christian word for 'God' is the Persian 'Khuda'. Yet for a Muslim the most natural word for God is 'Allah'.

Despite the obvious disappointments in a pastoral ministry I have never lost heart. I remember on July 17th, 1973, when I came to Sukkur the Lord spoke to me clearly as He did to Jeremiah the Old Testament prophet. 'I chose you even before you were born.' I have always had the assurance that God would help me in this ministry and this has kept me going. But there have been encouraging moments too. My relationship with some of my parishioners became so close that an almost telepathic communication developed between us. There was Josephine who came from a very poor family. Her father worked in a cement factory. When she matriculated from high school, Daisy and I decided to send her to Hyderabad to do nursing. On her graduation the manager of the cement factory gave her a job in the factory hospital. She was also given a house. In Pakistan it is common to find various organisations with their own hospitals. In addition there are the mission hospitals and the state hospitals. Josephine naturally had a very close relationship with our family. One Tuesday morning I woke with the compelling sense that I must go and see her. I had seen her and her family on the previous Sunday and it was difficult to convince Daisy that I should go again. Anyway I went. I found her with a temperature of 103°F and her father, very distressed, sitting on her bed. They had been hoping and praying that I would arrive. I prayed for her and within fifteen minutes she was serving us tea!

Something similar happened in 1974. I woke up one morning at 1 a.m. and began thinking of a family I knew. The man was an electrician and worked on the railways. For no obvious reason I felt that his wife needed me. Without waking the family, I got up, took my motorbike and went to the house of a young helper in the parish, my catechist. Needless to say he was amazed to see me at that hour of the morning and even more surprised that I should expect him to get dressed and come with me. Reluctantly, he came and we found that the wife, who had acute asthma, could not breathe properly. Once again she too had been praying for me to go and see her. I prayed for her and she recovered. She was a very sick woman however and within a few months she was dead. But she died peacefully.

Another of my parishioners, Shakuntala, was unwell and I visited her. I remember how she pleaded with me not to go far away because she said she needed me. I was going on a week's evangelistic tour to Nawabshah.

After two days there, I was convinced that I should return home. My assistant, George, was very puzzled. He had arranged a meeting for me. I could not possibly go to it. I could not explain the strong compulsion within me. It is not that I am the sort of person who would follow my feelings just for the sheer satisfaction of pleasing myself. Air Force discipline had taught me differently. Eventually I persuaded George that I had to go. When I arrived home Daisy was surprised and yet pleased to see me. She had tried unsuccessfully to contact me. Apparently Shakuntala had died that morning and she had made a last request: I must conduct her funeral. It seems that at the time I was experiencing the compulsion to return home was the time she was making her wish known.

I always seemed to be at the right place at the right time. Quite recently, I was in Karachi because I was the convener of a youth conference. While I was there I learnt that one of my faithful parishioners from Mirpur Khas, Simon, had died in Karachi to which he had been brought by his son. He wanted me to conduct his funeral and I was pleased that I was able to do so.

A Christian's funeral is a special occasion. It is not only for sentimental reasons that people desire their friends to be present. It is a time for witnessing to their Lord. Death opens the way for the Christian into the presence of his Lord. This is the hope which sustains him throughout his life. He wants to share it with others. He is able even at his death to witness to others. The Pastor has a unique opportunity of telling others who have no such hope or faith. In some ways it can be the beginning of an awakening in people's hearts. So I always rejoice at the opportunity of witnessing for my Lord even in distressing situations. It is not unusual for me to be called upon to share in the joys and sorrows of my people on a single day. I may perform a baptism in the morning and share in the joy of a newborn child of God; in the joyfulness and seriousness of a wedding in the afternoon and then in the mourning of a loved one in the evening. For me to 'weep with those who weep, mourn with those who mourn and rejoice with those who rejoice' is a constant reality.

I find in a pastoral situation that a lot of my time is taken up with the ceremonies associated with important junctures in people's lives. Baptisms usually provide plenty of opportunity of teaching the Christian faith though these are not without their amusing moments. Sometimes when I am conducting a service a mild argument arises between the parents. When I ask them to make the promises for the child, the father usually turns to me and says, 'Tell her, (i.e. the wife) that is her responsibility.' Then the wife would retort, 'Tell him, he is never at home.' Much restraint is often needed. But I always insist they make the promises together. Sometimes they even forget the name of the child to be baptised. One couple insisted that their daughter's name was 'Machine'. I had a hard time trying to convince them that it couldn't be and went through a whole lot of names which had the sound of 'machine'. Eventually, they agreed that the child's name was 'Shameen'!

From the beginning of my ministry I had always

been interested in the very poor. To me their need for the Gospel and their response to it have always been dear to my heart. I also felt an urgent need for education especially among the sweeper class. The latter group are the last to encourage their children to go to school. They believe that there will always be a sweeper's job for them. They fail to see that as technology advances, there will be fewer manual or unskilled jobs left. My main concern here was to convince the young men. Education is their only hope. With some persuasion I was able to get the diocese of Sind to establish a hostel for some of these boys. Daisy has been of immense help to me in this area of my work. People respect her and listen to her.

Soon after we arrived here Daisy was offered a job in the Mission hospital. She worked three days a week for one year but then the hospital was closed. Such was her reputation however that she received an offer from the government to start a school of nursing in a civil hospital in Sukkur. In this very influential position she was able to witness to her student nurses, many of whom were converted. She encouraged them to pray with their patients and to establish good relationships with their relatives. The hospital authorities made no objection to her adding this Christian dimension to her work because she was giving such valuable service. However, the downfall came soon enough. In 1978 she went to a conference on leadership training in evangelism in Singapore. This heralded the end of her work for the government. Three weeks after her return she received notice of termination of her employment. No reasons were given. Despite much encouragement from her friends to petition the government she accepted her dismissal and trusted her Lord to provide for her.

Within a month of her leaving that job she was offered the position of a Nursing Superintendent in a private hospital. This she accepted as a God-given appointment. Soon after, however, a disagreement arose over the question of leave. She had been accustomed to forego her leave on various occasions so that she could go to Christian meetings and conferences when they were held. Her bosses did not approve: her attendance at conferences disrupted the smooth running of the hospital. In the end she had to leave, surrendering a month's salary. She left in July 1983. We still believe that God does provide for us but He does not safeguard us against the evil designs of men. We must take our share in suffering humanity. In the providence of God she was not left in this position for very long. In September the Bishop of the Diocese offered her the job of organising the prayer groups and fellowship meetings in the Diocese with the result that once again she is gainfully employed in the Lord's business.

It is my strong belief that God cares for the whole man and therefore I do not restrict my work to preaching the Gospel and taking services in church. Daisy and I have established a clinic in one of the Bastees (this is the name given to the areas where the very poor live). Together with some volunteers we go each week to see mothers and their children. We help them with prescriptions for medicines and teach them how to care for their children. It is always so sad to find that with poverty goes lack of education and basic hygiene. Our women volunteers are a great help in this. They demonstrate to the women how to prepare meals for their children and how to keep

151

their houses clean. We also have a service during which time we teach them the rudiments of the Christian faith. Some have been converted, and to see the growth in their faith gives us much cause for rejoicing. Usually they are more influential in bringing their friends and neighbours to the Lord than we are.

Daisy has truly been my 'helpmeet'. With her encouragement and help all through the years I think I have managed to remain faithful to God, my deliverer; and He has always been faithful and supplied all our needs. Our great joy has been to see the Kingdom of God grow and to be privileged to share in its work. Even our earthly joys have not been overlooked. Although we do not have a house of our own, we have watched with delight the way our Father has blessed our household. Our children have grown up as beautiful plants in the sunshine of His love.

Our eldest son Samuel, for whose birth we prayed and whom we dedicated to the Lord has given his life to Christ. Having finished his BSc in social work he now works as a Christian evangelist. Quite recently with the help of some local young Christians he arranged a Christian literature distribution campaign in Sukkur. Posters were put up all over the town and for a whole week Sukkur seemed to be talking of nothing else but the Christian faith. Samuel continues to study for his Master's degree. Self-sacrifice forms part of a beautifully developing character. When he discovered that we could not afford to keep him in college, he decided to study privately, so that his sister could go to medical college. Here is another tale of rejoicing for us. After our daughter Kuldah had her interview for entrance to medical college, we heard nothing from the medical school. In Pakistan people use their influence and status to get their children into educational institutions. We had no one except our God. But having Him is to have everything. Shortly before the term started we received a letter from the medical school asking why Kuldah had not responded to the offer of a place at the school. We of course knew nothing of such an offer. We had received no letter. Maybe it got lost in the post. We were very surprised because such an offer would not normally be left open for months in view of the fierce competition there is to enter medical training. We were reminded of the words of the psalmist, 'The Lord is protector of my share.' Kuldah is now in her fourth year at college and will qualify as a doctor in 1985. Praise the Lord!

Our second son, Obed Nayer, has finished his BSc. He too has dedicated himself to our Lord although as yet he does not know what work the Lord has in store for him.

What a blessing it is to have a Christian household. In the early days of Christianity, whole households were converted. To be able to share with one another our experiences of the Lord is very enriching. For me the greatest joy is that my children carry the message of salvation, of cleansing and healing, in their family name—Naaman.

I would not want to give the impression, however, that my domestic life has been perfect. Satan never misses an opportunity to make mischief. There have been times when the very foundation of our marriage and household was severely threatened and collapse seemed inevitable. Because women more often than men responded to my evangelistic message, there were those who were unscrupulous enough to plant seeds of distrust in Daisy's mind. For example, one lady in my congregation was very ill and needed a blood transfusion. I asked my son Samuel, who was of the same blood group, to give his and this he did willingly. Unfortunately, according to Eastern thinking, this was my blood being given, and the repercussions for me were most unpleasant. The lady recovered but instead of being grateful she exploited the situation and made my family life most uncomfortable. Other women took advantage of the spiritual relationships which I was trying to foster with them and their families as members of my congregation to make Daisy jealous and naturally suspicious. Sometimes she would become very depressed and embittered but by God's help we have managed to weather these storms. Such experiences do leave scars on all of us.

Our time in Sukkur has also been marked by financial hardship. We have been robbed several times but we have not gone to the police because we know that the culprits will be severely beaten and this we did not want. Sometimes my 'old Adam' becomes alive and tries to force me to get my property recovered but I have to recrucify him so that he does not lead me to displease my master Jesus.

As my ministry here in Sukkur draws to a close, I reflect with great satisfaction on the way the Lord has led me. I know that I am not perfect and have probably made many mistakes.

'The enemy has often tugged at our skirt
But has never succeeded in beguiling us.'

In my heart I know that my first love has always been for evangelism rather than a pastoral ministry. Not that there is no room for evangelism in a pastoral ministry. There certainly is, but this is only a part of it. My God, however, has led me in the path He has chosen for me and I have submitted. I knew that only in this way could I live my life to His glory. I owe it all to Him who first loved me and set His love upon me. In my own strength I could have done nothing. But all I am, and all I have been able to do, have been accomplished only through His working in me.

The road to my 'Calvary' has been a thorny one. It was worse than I had expected. But I knew all the time that a certain young man, Jesus of Nazareth, had walked this way before me. This thought gave me strength and kept me going even when the weight of my 'cross' also seemed to be too much for me. I was constantly reminded of His words; 'If any man would come after me, let him deny himself and take up his cross and follow me' (Mark 8:34). For me this was the only path I could tread, the only way I could serve Him and bring others to the foot of the Cross. It was my response to His great love for me.

The path of service is also a lonely one. Sometimes this self-imposed loneliness can be misunderstood as when for weeks and even months on end I find no enjoyment in the conversation and company of other people. But it is at these times that I am able to identify closely with my Lord and Master. Dying for Christ in this life enables me to experience also the power of His resurrection. In Him I experience, while still in this life, the victory of life over death.

A great poet of Pakistan, Sir Mohammed Iqbal, has defined life and death as, 'Life is the name of an

155

order in the visible things; death is when this order is broken and scattered.' After I left my Muslim (extended) family of forty-two members, I found it hard to adjust to my new circumstances. I had kind sisters-in-law who had shown me much love; a mother who never spoke a harsh word to me or to anyone in my presence; a father whose gracious personality was a shining example to me and who provided me with wise guidance; my four brothers who were always concerned about my well being and who always wanted to see me a happy young man but who unfortunately became my bitter enemies. Life without them seemed very bewildering. Even my best Muslim friends who always valued my friendship and faithfulness became strangers to me. Such friend-ships had been forged in very difficult situations. I remember one occasion when, as a freedom fighter, I was in charge of an operation on the Kashmir border. We were in the midst of fighting. Gun fire was being exchanged from both sides. My friend Akbar Kazmi found his rifle had jammed. He was terrified. It was like being unarmed. I watched him and saw the look of hopelessness on his face. I threw my own rifle to Kazmi to use for his defence. I felt that I did not need it as much since I was a strong young man and knew how to protect myself without any weapons. This action cemented our friendship. When my family began to persecute me, even a close friend like Kazmi was unable to do anything to help me. Devoid of relatives and friends I had to find my own way in life. It was like a 'social death' to me. Yet I kept on walking on the road I had chosen.

'To die daily' for our Lord is not a promise one should undertake lightly. I have not regretted making mine. When I see lives changed and blessed, it has been a great joy to me. But there have been discouraging moments when my labour has seemed to be in vain. When I see young women I have helped to educate and bring up in the Christian faith, abandoning all to become second wives of Muslim men I get very distressed and depressed. I am soon reminded however that our Lord Himself died for all and yet so few respond to His love. Then I ask myself, 'What is my love and labour compared to His?' His self-sacrifice on the Cross was seen as weakness. When I am abused and do not retaliate, I am also accused of being weak. I cannot expect to be treated any differently to my Master.

I am now ready when He calls me 'to change my old clothes and put on new ones'. I know that for a Christian death is not the end of life, but the beginning of a new and better one. After I am gone from this world, I shall have no chance to 'die daily' for Him. In one sense it will be a loss to me as I have gained much by being crucified with Him. While I am in this body, on this side of heaven, I am able to bring others to Him. I can encourage many to walk in this world with confidence and glorify my Master's name and praise Him. My Lord and my God has led me faithfully all my years. I know that my defeats have been His defeats and my victories have been His victories. Praise His Name!

I do earnestly hope that God has accepted my 'priestly ministry' of winning souls for Him. A few years ago I went to a Diocesan meeting in Karachi and I saw Manzur and Dadu officiating at the Eucharist at Holy Trinity Cathedral. I bowed my head in thanksgiving and praise and when I received the blessed sacrament at their hands such a thrill went through me that I almost felt my heart would burst with joy! I had been instrumental in bringing both these men to the Lord. What more could an unworthy servant desire?

> 'The person who is annihilated worshipping at
>   your threshold
> Becomes a means of worship to others.'

So I thank God that He met me as the enemy I did not expect. My prayer is that those who read of Him in this book will be numbered among the saints who praise Him in everlasting light.

If you wish to receive *regular information* about *new books,* please send your name and address to:

London Bible Warehouse
PO Box 123
Basingstoke
Hants RG23 7NL

Name _____

Address _____

_____

_____

_____

I am especially interested in:

☐ Biographies
☐ Fiction
☐ Christian living
☐ Issue related books
☐ Academic books
☐ Bible study aids
☐ Children's books
☐ Music
☐ Other subjects

P.S. If you have ideas for new Christian Books or other products, please write to us too!